What people are saying about

Not for Nothing

So much written on religious issues these days is second rate and derivative, that it's good to have a robust independent voice with an optimistic, realistic, coherent, accessible and well-written take on faith.

Canon Angela Tilbey, Canon Emeritus at Christ Church, Oxford. Author, *Soul: God, Self and New Cosmology*

Peter Armstrong has provided us with a thoughtful and thoroughly readable account of his lifelong attempts to make sense of his Christian faith in the modern world. His 'heretical' perspectives on Jesus actually present a very appealing understanding of who He was and is.

May his honesty and courage inspire many to take the next steps on their own pilgrimage to truth.

The Rt. Rev. C. Christopher Epting VIII Bishop of Iowa (Ret.) The Episcopal Church

Not for Nothing

Searching for a meaningful life

Not for Nothing

Searching for a meaningful life

Peter Armstrong

Winchester, UK
Washington, USA

JOHN HUNT PUBLISHING

First published by Christian Alternative Books, 2020
Christian Alternative Books is an imprint of John Hunt Publishing Ltd.,
No. 3 East St., Alresford, Hampshire SO24 9EE, UK
office@jhpbooks.com
www.johnhuntpublishing.com
www.christian-alternative.com

For distributor details and how to order please visit the 'Ordering' section on our website.

Cover photograph: Harald Löffel

ISBN: 978 1 78904 296 2
978 1 78904 297 9 (ebook)
Library of Congress Control Number: 2019948222

A CIP catalogue record for this book is available from the British Library.

Design: Stuart Davies

UK: Printed and bound by CPI Group (UK) Ltd, Croydon, CR0 4YY
US: Printed and bound by Thomson-Shore, 7300 West Joy Road, Dexter, MI 48130

Contents

This small book is dedicated in heartfelt gratitude to my mother Gwen, who brought me up in the faith; my father William, who gave me the courage to question everything from first principles; Leslie Houlden, who introduced me to the wider church; my first philosophy tutor, Anthony Kenny; Brother Roger, who welcomed me to Taizé; my precious daughter Boo, entrusted to God; George Caird, who opened up the New Testament; John Lang, my patron at the BBC; Dom Hélder Câmara, who showed me a new path to global justice; Don Cupitt, my mentor in critical theology; Franz Schubert the musical companion of my later years; and so many others. But above all to my wife Anuradha from whom I learnt all I know about the wisdom of the heart and the meaning of true love.

Foreword

Not for nothing have we lived.

For an optimistic book the early twenty-first century doesn't feel like a promising time to start writing. The news on climate change grows daily worse, as time runs out to take the necessary steps to avoid catastrophe for our planet. Politically, fascism is on the rise as dangerous clowns take hold of the levers of power from the US to the Philippines, from Italy to Brazil. And the simple contradiction at the heart of our consumer society – that we can have endless economic growth on a finite planet – remains something we just don't want to think about, much less deal with. All this in spite of the heroic, lifelong efforts of so many inspiring activists who have given their lives to fight for a better world. 'Say not the struggle naught availeth' – and keep remembering that, because just at the moment it doesn't seem to be availing at all.

And yet, I believe *not for nothing have we struggled.*

And writing an optimistic book in one's mid-seventies can seem equally unpromising. Old men should be explorers, said T.S. Eliot, but it becomes harder to keep up the momentum as physical and mental powers decline and the final deadline looms. But I am determined to try to explain something of what I have learned along my personal journey: in and out of the church, too long at Oxford studying philosophy, psychology and theology, fifty years making films to try to capture some of the best insights of my generation.

Because I hope *not for nothing have I lived.*

And yet, and yet. This is an optimistic book because, in spite of these negatives, I find myself loving life more than ever, feeling more strongly than ever its deep meaningfulness. In spite of all the evidence, you might well say. And this comes down to the set of beliefs I have finally arrived at: an idiosyncratic

way of thinking and being that I want to explore here. These hard-won beliefs will have to prove tough-minded if they are to provide real answers to the problems we all face. Facile hope and unthinking religion won't cut it.

Not for nothing have I remained a Christian.

Christianity is today increasingly thought of as make-believe: an outworn creed without hard evidence to back it up. I agree. I agree, that is, in the sense that religion is made up: it is a totally human creation. And I agree about the lack of hard evidence. But I do not dismiss it for that reason, because many things that we humans create are created for deeper reasons than describing the everyday world. Just ask Beethoven or Shakespeare.

Of course there are Christians and Christians: televangelists and desert monks, theologians in ivory towers and priests in *favelas*, devout Catholic grandmothers and followers of end-of-the-world cults. They share a common name though their beliefs are not only different but often utterly opposed. Catholics burned Protestants and Protestants tortured Catholics. So I'm going to have to be careful to establish where I fit into this maelstrom of beliefs, and indeed whether I deserve the label of Christian at all. I need to discover whether there is a place to stand with integrity, somewhere on the spectrum from unthinking fundamentalism at one end to outright atheism at the other. For me it needs to be somewhere that acknowledges fully the shared conclusions of today's scientific worldview, while at the same time responding to the spiritual hunger experienced by many people stuck in today's hollow consumer society.

Whom am I writing for? I guess for myself – to try and articulate what I believe and what I don't. Then perhaps for the children and grandchildren. Hence the informal style that's emerging – chatty even – as I try to put into words, I hope are not too pompous ideas that are hard for me to bring into coherence, let alone explain to others. But I want to try.

These pages will be about feelings more than arguments,

belief more than knowledge, pictures more than propositions, love more than rules. Above all, they will be about a search for meaning. I think what I will end up saying by the end of this short book is a list of very simple things: that the universe is ultimately benign, that love is all, that human failings can be forgiven, that there is life beyond death, and that this whole cosmos has ultimate meaning. And if you ask me what that meaning is, I think I'm going to finally conclude: love that lasts.

Hedgerley Wood
2019

Well, Are You a Christian or Aren't You?

In the Universe there are things that are known and things that are unknown, and in between there are doors.[1]
Anon.

The stupidest thing that that very wise man Carl Jung said, when asked if he believed in God, was: 'I do not need to believe, I *know*.'[2]

If that's the test, then I am certainly not a Christian. I don't *know* there is a God. I don't *know* there is life after death – or any of the rest of the big Christian metaphysical superstructure. Perfect knowledge implies certainty, resting on some logical proof. Even the claim to everyday knowing requires at least some evidence that cannot be gainsaid. It is clear to me, as to more and more people, that neither philosophical proof nor empirical evidence for the existence of God is available. I cannot claim to know the truth of any of the traditional, metaphysical claims of Christianity.

'So, you are an agnostic?'

Yes, but a Christian agnostic. I don't *know* there is God, but I *believe in* God. The exact opposite of Jung's affirmation.

Belief is going to be a central idea in this book, and I will be taking it in two very different senses.

In the first sense, I *believe* a proposition to be true if I think it is true even though I do not know for certain that it is true. 'I believe Arsenal will win on Saturday.' I may have some reason for my belief, but I have no certainty.

The second sense of the word is much deeper, leaning on the meaning of the Greek word used for 'I believe' in the New Testament: πιστεύω. This is belief in the sense of believing in, or trusting. 'I believe in you, I have faith in you.' 'I believe in Arsenal in spite of recent results.' In many societies, religious

people are called 'believers'.

I'll be focusing on this sense of *believing in* God – trusting God, having faith in God – later in the book, but I'll begin with the simpler of idea of *believing that* something is the case. So my claim as a Christian agnostic is that I don't *know* that God exists but I *believe* that God exists.

We are not starting on very firm ground with this kind of religious belief. Since we no longer live with heresy trials and do not yet have thought police, believing things can be relatively cost free. I could, for a Puckish example, believe in fairies without having to show any evidence for their existence. You can challenge the rationality of my belief but you cannot demonstrate that I do not believe it. Or I can decide today that I believe in fairies and tomorrow decide that I no longer do. Such beliefs carry little cost beyond mild ridicule. And even that ridicule can be avoided if I don't tell anyone I believe in fairies.

So, just because there is little cost, I've got to be careful to be true to myself and not just claim to believe this or that for no reason. I will hope to show that I *have* reasons for my beliefs – although as Blaise Pascal, one of my philosophical heroes, put it, my reasons are not reasons of the head but reasons of the heart. I will hope to show that a belief can be reasonable, even when not based on empirical evidence. It's quite possible to believe more than you know. I can quote a distinguished philosopher on this point. Anthony Kenny, one of my Oxford tutors, put it like this: 'It is possible to have good reasons for believing in a proposition quite separate from reasons that provide evidence for its truth.'[3] Why you would do that is another question that we will come to later.

The second snare that awaits me is to set up belief (in this first sense of believing that particular religious doctrines are true) as the criterion for whether I am a Christian or not. In traditional forms of Christianity this orthodoxy check is the very test for salvation, for avoiding eternal damnation. The central creed, recited in many churches every Sunday, is so called because it begins 'Credo – I believe.' And the Athanasian form of the creed ends with the words: 'This is the Catholic Faith; unless anyone believes this faithfully and firmly, he cannot be saved.'

I can't accept that I have to subscribe to any formula or list of beliefs (like the creeds or the 39 Articles of the Church of England) in order to justify my claim to be a Christian. My beliefs are no more than my personal way of looking at and understanding the world, using the language and images of the particular religious culture with which I have been imbued. Moreover, I need to feel free to adjust, expand or abandon some beliefs as my experience of life changes and deepens. I can't join any club that insists on fixed creeds and belief systems. That would be to surrender my essential freedom as an autonomous individual: to be forced into an institutional mould. Nor should you be forced into my mould. For me, my particular beliefs help make sense of life but they may not do so for you.

This approach to believing is not the same as 'taking it on faith'. In ordinary usage what people mean by this is something like: 'Ok, you think I'm crazy to believe that God exists, but you have to take it on faith.' And that in turn means: 'Because that's what the Church teaches or God has revealed in the Bible.' But that is hardly convincing. There's a contradiction built into the argument. If God doesn't exist, then the Bible can't be relied upon as the word of God to prove that He does exist. To quote Anthony Kenny, again: 'Accepting something as a matter of faith is taking God's word for its truth: but one cannot take God's word for it that He exists.'[4]

So being clear that I can't claim to *know* all the things that I believe to be true helps me understand something I used to have a problem with: why so many people describe themselves as 'seekers' when it comes to religion. That used to sound like a cop-out: 'I'm not really Christian or Muslim, but I am a seeker.' But now I see that being a seeker, a life-pilgrim, means seeing that the final answers to the religious questions are never found, the destination is never reached. For Christians at the fundamentalist end of the spectrum, certainty is exactly what they crave, and what they most value about religious belief. By contrast, as a Christian agnostic, I am forever seeing through a glass darkly, forever guessing God, aware that my guess is only a guess. As to knowing God, perhaps I can only hope, like St Paul, that in some world to come 'I shall know even as I am known.'[5]

I remember my father asking himself the same question I am wrestling with here: Are you a Christian or aren't you? He had come from a strict Salvation Army upbringing, through atheism at Oxford, to arrive at his own idiosyncratic form of belief. He put the issue like this:

> I would dearly love the leaders of the Church to say clearly and unequivocally how much of the traditional story and inherited doctrine they believe, how much they interpret away, how much they have mental reservations about, and how much they simply reject. I have tried to do this for myself and have arrived at a set of propositions that seem to me both to satisfy my intellect and to preserve my faith in Christ – but I do not have the faintest idea whether there is any Church on earth that would accept me as a Christian. It would be nice to know: but I do not think I should presume to ask for it. I am content – almost content – to leave that to the Holy Spirit… I have scattered seeds that I believe to be good, but I cannot be sure: I can only leave them to your judgement as I offer them to the greater glory of God.[6]

So to characterize my position as a Christian agnostic I go back to the quotation at the head of the chapter. 'There are things that are known.' Yes, that's the world of science and everyday life. 'And things that are unknown.' Yes, and some of the unknowns that are crucial to the meaning of our lives may be true. We can't know that they are true, but we can believe that they are true. 'And in between there are doors.' Yes, these are the doors I want to encounter and walk through: to have the faith and trust in the goodness of existence to believe that, if I try those doors, they will open onto a world of meaning and the fullness of joy.

A footnote on Carl Jung. To be fair to him, he wasn't really being as simplistic as I was suggesting earlier. He explained later that he was speaking of God as an inner experience. In his *Red Book,* where he explored his 'confrontation with the unconscious', he put it like this:

> I believe that we have the choice: I preferred the living wonders of the God. I daily weigh up my whole life and I continue to fiery brilliance of the God as a higher and fuller life than the ashes of rationality. The ashes are suicide to me. I could perhaps put out the fire but I cannot deny to myself the experience of the God. Nor can I cut myself off from this experience. I also do not want to, since I want to live. My life wants itself whole.[7]

My Starting Point

There is a grace in life. Otherwise we could not live.[1]
Paul Tillich

If I am aiming so arrogantly as to begin the account of what I believe *de novo,* without relying on the traditional foundational arguments of the past, what starting point can I take?

I want to begin at the point that both Marx and Freud regarded as religion's Achilles heel – my need for God. Put simply, I cannot believe that my life and the life of the world are simply meaningless: that my life is a tale told by an idiot, lasting a fraction of cosmic time before being snuffed out and ultimately signifying nothing. I *need* life to mean something, a reason to be here, a reason to keep going, a reason to get up in the morning, even on a morning when I have absolutely nothing else left in life to look forward to. Otherwise life feels like it's *for nothing*.

The protagonist in William Boyd's novel *The New Confessions* expresses the same starting point as he reaches the age that I've now reached:

> I look back on my life, my three score years and ten, and think – yes, I would like there to be an underlying order to these seven decades of reality. I would like some sense, some meaning. But science, which used to attempt to enumerate all the cogs in the Great Machine, has abandoned that endeavour now. Life at its basic level, the quantum physicists tell us, is deeply paradoxical and fundamentally uncertain. There are no hidden variables, there is no secret agenda to the universe.[2]

This is the same question as the one that must occur to most of us at some point in our life: 'Is this all there is?' We are born, we live for the tiniest fraction of cosmic space-time and we die. Is that it? Must we all, as Dr. Johnson puts it, simply 'yield our place to others who, like us, shall be driven awhile by hope or fear, about the surface of the earth, and then like us be lost in the shades of death.'[3] Is that all there is?

Life is frighteningly short. I made the mistake of going back to my Oxford college for a reunion after 50 years. That evening I met students whom I had known well, who had started off on life full of excitement but had now suddenly switched into old men, retired and looking back on lives that were, in effect, over. That's it – over. I'm writing this page on Patmos, an island I last came to aged 21 to explore what my life was going to be. Now I'm back for the first time exactly 50 years later with the same quest, and very aware that I won't be back in another 50 years. Life is ludicrously short – just when we were beginning to get the hang of it.

And it's human consciousness that makes our brief moment on life's stage so poignant. The cows outside my window at home seem contented enough to eat their way through each day without anxiety, unaware that they are due to be slaughtered at the end of the year. But we are all too aware of our mortality. And the same consciousness that knows it also seems to rebel against it, raging at the dying of the light, unwilling to accept as we get older that this is all there is.

There are two levels to the issue of meaningfulness that I am struggling with here. Firstly, does the universe have any meaning? Here the answer from science is clear: it has no meaning. There is no goal or purpose to the universe. It just *is*, in its vast, beautiful, possibly infinite, pointless way. The so-called 'first bible of atheism', *The System of Nature* by Baron D'Holbach, makes this clear: 'The world itself has neither point nor purpose of its own. It just is.'[4]

So what of the second level – the meaning of my life or yours? This personal meaning can't be discovered by looking at my place in the universe, if the universe itself is meaningless. So we'll have to come up with meanings of our own. Here there are dozens of answers being offered me. They range from being as happy as possible for as long as possible, to having children to succeed me, to leaving a better world behind me, to reaching a high level of consciousness, to sacrificing my life as a martyr, to leaving a legacy in the arts or letters, and many more. These are all notions that clearly help some people feel that their life is meaningful some of the time. What they all have in common is that they are subjective, they are the kinds of meanings that I would assign to my life myself. The only test they need to pass is whether they make me *feel* that my life is meaningful. There is no solid ground on which these self-assigned meanings rest. What is offered is *a* meaning for my life: not *the* meaning. If I try and describe this sense of a meaningful life in more objective terms, then I face a bleak response from secular science. Is my life on the right track? There is no right track. Am I following my vocation? There is no voice to call you to anything. What is the true purpose of my life? There is no true purpose. I may have invented a track or a vocation or a purpose for my life, but these are only as good as they make me feel.

So, if I want to find a rational basis for the meaning of my life, the question becomes: Can I believe that my life is meaningful in the context of a meaningless world? And for me the answer is No. I might try and persuade myself of some meaning or other that I devise myself, or one devised by the society around me, but for me that isn't enough to make my life meaningful. For that, my life's meaning has to derive from the meaningfulness of the world. And that's clearly not on offer from secular science.

I don't think anyone would disagree with my starting points: that we feel a deep need for meaning in our lives, and the picture of the world that a straightforward scientific viewpoint presents to us is of a world with no meaning. Beyond that, what I am claiming is that attempts to invent meanings aren't enough. They don't seem to me to provide solid grounds for believing and feeling that my life is meaningful, with a meaning that can survive all life's dark days.

Perhaps the clearest attempt to wrestle with these questions of meaning is the philosophy of existentialism. Humans, Jean-Paul Sartre said, cannot bear the utter meaninglessness of the cosmos and the only way to respond is with heroic acceptance of life as an absurdity without any meaning. He claimed to be undaunted by this meaninglessness, choosing freely to enjoy existence as a life-long theatre of the absurd. I entirely agree with his view that life is absurd seen only from the standpoint of secular science. But, unlike Sartre, I am not content to live in a universe that I consider absurd. I agree with Sartre's fellow existentialist, Albert Camus, that we are faced with an existential choice: on what basis we choose to live our lives, or indeed whether it is worth living at all. Camus wrote: 'There is but one serious philosophical problem and that is suicide. Judging whether life is or is not worth living amounts to answering the fundamental question of philosophy.'[5]

Once, filming in the heartbreaking slums of India, one of the UK party with me said: 'If I had to live like this, I would kill myself.' Maybe that is the bleak logic of our mortality and the suffering of the world. I might be tempted by the *carpe diem* slogan. Let's live only for the day, enjoy life so long as it is satisfying for us personally and, as soon as the days ahead offer only pain and suffering, time for euthanasia. A doctor friend who works in the hospice movement said to us this week: 'I believe the wide acceptance of assisted dying is becoming inevitable.'

A shocking survey in 2018 by YouGov[6] in the UK found that 18 per cent of young people between 16 and 25 years old do not think life is worth living. More than 25 per cent of them reported that their life had no sense of purpose. This may well reflect the context of austerity and climate anxiety that young people face today, but it may be more than that – the sense that the meanings

being offered by Western society for giving our lives meaning are becoming less and less persuasive.

'Stop being so gloomy!' I hear you protesting. 'I enjoy plenty of things about life and they provide me with all the meaning I need: my work, art, my children and much more.' I'm pleased for you, but personally I need this everyday sense of meaning to have deeper roots – a deeper underlying sense of ultimate meaning to support it. My starting point for everyday life is the same as yours – that life feels meaningful – but if I were an atheist, I would have to be satisfied with whatever form of meaning I could come up with in the face of a meaningless world.

That takes us to the next step of my thinking, the strong *feeling* that I already have that life is meaningful, not just in a subjective way, but that it has an *ultimate* meaningfulness derived from outside myself, from a meaningful universe. That is my premise. It is not based on any evidence – quite the contrary. I just don't experience life on a daily basis as meaningless. It feels purposeful. It feels as though investing time in learning and improving my capabilities is worthwhile. It feels that none of this is absurd or just destined to be thrown away when I die. I feel the world has meaning. I feel my life has meaning. I feel the universe is meaningful. Only feelings, yes, but they are what I feel. Moreover, they are what I need to feel in order to keep on through the trials and tribulations of daily life – and past the barrier of death. This is the only way I can make sense of the beauty, human creativity and deep, deep love that I feel is central to my life. Are all these things meaningless: the tiniest flicker of insignificant activity in a universe of a trillion stars? They may be, but I couldn't live as though they were.

My position is nothing to do with evidence. It is everything to do with arriving at a personal worldview that is not self-contradictory. I would be contradicting myself if I tried to believe both that the world is meaningful and that secular science is the whole story. As I was coming up with titles for this book, one I

liked was 'Letter to Horatio', filling out the thought that 'there is more in heaven and earth than is dreamt of in your philosophy, Horatio.'[7] Not that I start by knowing what this *more* is, just the sense that there must be more. What is this immense firmament of the heavens with its billions of galaxies for? Does it have a purpose at all? Is there a goal for the cosmos? There seems to be an awful lot of it, if it's not for anything! When the psalmist sang 'When I survey the heavens...' he was drawn to the question 'What is man?' Whereas I feel more strongly the corollary. When I survey the unimaginable vastness and beauty of the universe, I can't help asking: 'What are these heavens? Can they be for nothing?' Either the cosmos has some meaning, which we have to account for somehow, or it has no meaning and we must resign ourselves to meaninglessness. That is the choice.

There are obvious objections to the position I am adopting. You may well ask, for example, whether my feelings are more than wish fulfillment. Wouldn't we all like it, you might suggest, if there were an answer to the life, the universe and everything? Other than 42. But if wishes were horses, beggars would ride. Samuel Wells, the Rector of St Martin in the Fields, puts his objection to my approach like this: 'These arguments are in the end useless, because it's a long way from saying that people need meaning, to any sense that those meanings are true.'[8] Agreed. But, as I have argued, I am resting my case not on things that are provably true, but things that are believable.

Moreover, the fact that I *want* to feel that my life is meaningful, that I have clear motivation for the set of beliefs that flow from that feeling, doesn't thereby disqualify my beliefs. The hero may be heroic to impress his parents. The comedian may be funny out of a childhood fear of rejection. The writer may write deathless prose to win prizes. But whether they are aware of these motivations or not, this does not diminish the power of their work or the authenticity of the personal philosophy that they live by. As Francis Spufford puts it, very neatly: 'If something

does exist, then wishing for that something does not infect it with wishfulness.'[9] I feel secure in my feeling that life just cannot be meaningless: that the things I value and the people that I love cannot be for nothing.

Nor do I deny the validity of other people's very different responses to this same reality. Sartre can discuss inventing God in order to be free to deny him. Camus can discuss the rationality of suicide in the face of the absurd. Many take drugs for pleasure or drugs to forget. And many seem able, in a way that I am not, to follow a Buddhist path where living in the moment with full mindfulness of suffering and death leads to the enlightened nothingness of nirvana. Each is a different response to an existential choice we all have to make: who am I, and on what basis am I to live my life? They are all possible human responses to the same reality, but they are not mine. To emphasize the point, I certainly don't want to deny a sense of a meaningful life to those people who are able to find it simply in living the here and now for as long as it lasts; finding meaning in family, work, planet Earth or whatever. It is just that for me that is not by itself enough, because I can't believe that my life is meaningful in the context of a meaningless world.

Now comes the crucial step. The observable world, the world as described by secular science, doesn't seem consistent with any meaning that satisfies me. And yet in spite of that, life feels meaningful and my life feels worth living to the full. So what extra dimensions must there be that would fit with this conviction of mine? There must be 'something more' if I am not to abandon my sense of meaning. Something more than the empty, pointless universe of secular scientific rationality. If I am to believe there is meaning and that life is worth living, that there exists love for which it's worth giving up everything, then what cosmic framework would be sufficient to be consonant with that meaning? That question is the heart of my faith – **if I can only live my life on the basis that the world has ultimate meaning**

and purpose, then what cosmic framework must there be in order to be the foundation of that meaning and purpose? To that foundation of meaning and purpose I give the name God – the unknowable God. This is the central point I want to make in writing this book. God's existence is not a provable fact, rather it is the hypothesis that makes sense of any trust in the ultimate meaningfulness of our lives. And after that, everything we go on to say about God is poetry.

Perhaps an analogy will help me explain what I mean by the idea of God being a hypothesis that makes sense of my experience. Suppose Robinson Crusoe is noticing that Man Friday is growing more and more resentful of him. But then Man Friday dies before he can ask him why. With no one else on the island and no other way to check what the reasons were, Robinson can only conjecture. What could the situation have been that would be consistent with the resentment he picked up? He comes up with a hypothesis that could explain it – Man Friday had resented his racism. But he cannot check. He can never know if his hypothesis is true. But he believes it and it makes sense of his world and his worldview. And he acts differently when Woman Saturday arrives on the island.

A feeble analogy perhaps. I'm not saying there must be God in order to give my life meaning. I am saying I experience my life as meaningful, so to be consistent I must believe in a background reality against which that feeling of meaning makes sense. And that reality I call the unknown God. The only alternative would be to revert to the idea that the world and my life are meaningless: and that would leave me feeling I had lived for nothing.

Let me try another analogy. The eighteenth-century French physicist Laplace famously told Napoleon that he had no need of the hypothesis of God to explain the mechanics of the solar system. And that view has rightly prevailed every time theologians have argued for a god of the gaps: God as an explanation for unsolved

puzzles in the scientific story. But science has its own need for hypotheses without evidence. Look at one of the greatest unsolved puzzles in today's cosmology: how our universe seems so perfectly tuned as to make life possible. In this case one of the explanations proposed by scientists themselves today is itself a pretty far out hypothesis: that our universe is just one universe in a multiverse, an infinite number of different universes in which all possible scientific laws are somewhere present. That's a big leap. There can be no direct evidence for the multiverse, but it is believable to some scientists because it explains the otherwise inexplicable. Their claim would be that there is 'a need for that hypothesis', even though it is not based on any evidence and can never be proved true or false. In the same way I rely on the God hypothesis to explain the meaningful world that I experience.

Once again, my argument is not about evidence but consistency. To be consistent I must believe that this God is real. An imaginary god who existed only in my head would not provide the cosmic framework I need. So I only have two logical choices: a real (unknown) God, or a meaningless universe.

I've been determined all the time I've been writing this book never to try and convert you or anyone else to my particular way of thinking. But then this afternoon I was listening to a podcast that gave me a moment of hesitation. Iain Dale was talking about his life as a politico and said this about God: 'I'm agnostic rather than atheist, because I can't prove that God doesn't exist and I can't prove He does exist, so I have to wait until someone can prove it one way or the other. If I'm honest, I've always kind of wanted to find religion, but no-one has ever managed to help me do so.'[10]

So perhaps I could at least offer to people like Iain the thought that, rather than having to give up on religion, it is possible to embrace something like the kind of agnostic approach to religion that I am describing without surrendering any intellectual integrity. You don't have to wait until someone 'proves it one way or the other', because God is not susceptible to proof. Instead you could start with the impulse, as Iain Dale describes it, to 'kind of want to find religion' and see where that leads you. I love the prayer of St Augustine: 'Thou hast made us for Thyself, and our hearts are restless until they find their rest in Thee.'[11]

Paths Not Taken

I do not know, dear reader, what your beliefs may be, but whatever they may be, you must concede that nine-tenths of the beliefs of nine-tenths of mankind are totally irrational. The beliefs in question are, of course, those which you do not hold.[1]
Bertrand Russell

This chapter is going to be less personal and more argumentative because it's about what I don't believe rather than what I do. People arrive at one of the Christian destinations from a number of different starting points. Most of them depend on some kind of appeal to authority: ready-made answers that we can take from our parents, our society, or the centuries of culture we have inherited.

Religion has a tendency to look to the past for authority. Science by contrast is open to the future. The days are long gone since scientists believed things because Aristotle taught them. But religion so often seems to takes its authority from old ideas: a sacred text or the remembered words of a prophet. Even 'new' ideas are often simply new interpretations of the original, like the relation of the Talmud to the Torah. Old stuff and, too often, fossilized thinking.

In a world that we see as increasingly strange and unexpected – with entangled quarks and the potential infinity of the multiverse – isn't it time to say to our religious ancestors, as Ibsen does in his play *Brand*: 'Your God is too small!'? That old God represented a good attempt for your time, but your categories and metaphors don't make sense in our world. Morally your tribal God of 2000 BCE who demands animal and human sacrifices is as abhorrent as your zero-tolerance God of 1500 CE who thinks heretics should be burned alive for not believing exactly the right detail of doctrine. And even today how can we respect an evangelical church version of a God who will damn us to eternal torment in Hell unless we profess the magic formula: 'I accept the Lord Jesus as my personal saviour.'

The same goes for much language and imagery from the past – which reminds me of that hilarious moment in the film *4 Weddings and a Funeral* when Rowan Atkinson, playing the vicar, pronounces: 'In the name of the Father and of the Son and of the Holy Goat.' But why is that so bizarre, when Blake has us all celebrating the 'Holy Lamb of God'? And *Agnus Dei* has been in Christian liturgies from the earliest days.

So much of such imagery goes back to animal sacrifices and it can be startling when looked at straight. I remember gazing solemnly at a stained-glass window and suddenly waking up and thinking, why are we celebrating a sheep bleeding into a cup? No wonder religion is so easy to mock, when its language and imagery are so easy to misunderstand. The impulse is strong to start again and try and find a path to faith that makes both literal and metaphoric sense for us today.

Among the most revered starting points are the philosophical 'proofs' of the existence of God, notably those set out in the cosmological arguments of Thomas Aquinas. Expressed in ordinary language they suggest arguments like: If everything is caused by something, then at the very beginning of the chain there must be something that has not been caused, i.e. God. Or again, there was the so-called ontological argument proposed by Anselm of Canterbury in the eleventh century CE. He argued that if God is the most perfect being imaginable, then He can't lack the quality of existence since then He would be thereby less perfect. Books and books have been written on these proofs and the conclusion seems unanimous that they do not hold water.

One possible exception is the recent attempt by some philosophers to refresh the cosmological argument by means of some of the latest scientific findings. A striking example comes from Professor Antony Flew, a philosopher famous in my time at Oxford as an atheist writing books like *The Presumption of Atheism*. But then he changed his mind completely, and in 2010 he published *There is a God*. He summarizes his new understanding like this:

> I now believe that the universe was brought into existence by an infinite Intelligence. I believe that this universe's intricate laws manifest what scientists have called the Mind of God. I believe that life and reproduction originate in a divine Source. Why do I believe this, given that I expounded and defended atheism for more than a half century? The short answer is this: this is the world picture, as I see it, that has emerged from modern science. Science spotlights three dimensions of nature that point to God. The first is the fact that nature obeys laws. The second is the dimension of life, of intelligently organized and purpose-driven beings, which arose from matter. The third is the very existence of nature.[2]

I am no scientist and in no position to make a judgement call on this. Scientists themselves are not rushing to endorse Flew's views, so until they do, I can't accept that there is a basis for this reinstatement of the old argument from Aquinas. The language games of natural science and supernatural religion seem to me too different for evidence from the first to prove anything in the second.

The next broad highway to faith is very straightforward, as long as you can accept the idea of direct revelation: the words that God Himself has spoken in a sacred text – the Bible, the Koran, the Book of Mormon, or wherever. This offers a simple shortcut to faith. For instance, 'The Christian doctrines are true because the Bible tells me so.'

Yesterday at Marylebone Station I was waiting in the coffee queue behind a fashionably dressed young woman reading a book. Surprisingly, it was entitled *Can I really Trust the Bible*?

Flipping through it now, I see its answer is: 'Yes, we can trust the Bible.' And why can we? The author describes the Old Testament as: 'The written records of the words of God as they were given by God, and as they were recorded by men who were specially designated and commanded by God to this work.'[3] Ah, so that's why.

I'd guess her book and many others like it will go on to claim that the Bible is inerrant: every word of it is true. Well, that might make faith easy to be certain about, as long as you don't mind the long list of contradictions between different Bible passages, and as long as you are happy to adopt the moral edicts that God apparently lays down in it, like never eating shellfish (Leviticus 11.12) and stoning to death anyone who commits adultery (Leviticus 20.10). I think most people would agree a belief in an inerrant Bible is hardly a convincing starting point for someone wondering whether or not to believe in God in the first place.

Another favourite jumping off point for many Christian apologists is human psychology; in particular human frailties, which religious traditions have promptly labelled as sins. This is the classic starting point that you will hear from practically every evangelical pulpit, where almost every sermon begins with the conviction of sin. I remember the huge crusades held by Billy Graham in the '50s and '60s. Graham's starting point for every address was to convict the audience of their personal sinfulness. 'All have sinned,' he would quote from the Epistle to the Romans, 'and fallen short of the glory of God.'[4] And he would spend the next half hour ensuring that we felt really guilty about something or other. Here is a compressed version of his sales pitch for Christianity at one of his campaign rallies in Anaheim, California, in 1969:

> There's a disease that's fatal to the whole human race – in the blood – called sin. And it has poisoned us. And the penalty is death… The Bible says you're the slave of sin… How many of

> you tonight are slaves of some habit? You're slaves of pride, slaves of jealousy… slaves of some secret sex sin that nobody knows anything about.
>
> Now how do we get purged from our sins?... You need atonement and there is only one way you can do it – through the blood… There is no forgiveness of sin outside the shedding of blood… Why the blood? Why does God demand blood? Remember that night in Egypt? When God said: 'I am going to destroy all the firstborn in Egypt as a judgement.' And He said, 'I want all you Israelites to take a lamb and slay the lamb, and then take the blood and sprinkle it on the doorposts. And when I see the blood I will pass over and I will not bring judgement on any house that has the blood there... And God was pointing to the day, hundreds of years in the future, when He would offer his own son, as the Lamb of God that taketh away the sins of the world.
>
> Tonight there is a blood bank that we can apply to by faith that will take our sin and our guilt away… Jesus Christ who died for you and gave his blood for you.[5]

In this way, Graham has set up an agreed problem – I am a sinner – to which he can then offer an answer – Jesus' blood shed on the cross to wipe away my sins. All I have to do is to come forward to the front of the arena in order to accept this atonement for my sin. It was a persuasive package, and in the heightened emotions of the moment it clearly worked for thousands of people each night of the campaign as they came to commit their lives to Jesus. Starting with sin worked.

But the sin starting point goes deeper than that. It wasn't only that I had sinned in all sorts of everyday ways, my sinfulness was much more deadly: I had been born with Original Sin, transmitted into my spiritual DNA from my first ancestors,

Adam and Eve.

The idea of original sin, developed most vividly by St Augustine in the fifth century CE, came to dominate the thinking of the Western church. And once again this form of sin and the guilt that follows from it are offered as primary reasons to accept the salvation offered by the Church as the only way out. But how acceptable does this offer seem now, when its whole approach runs counter to today's therapeutic orthodoxy that making people feel even more guilty than they already do is the last thing that will help them? Indeed, such guilt-tripping is, rightly in my view, seen as harmful. And in passing I might add that it is one reason why, when it comes to churches, I am attracted to the side of the Eastern Orthodox tradition that rejects the whole notion of original sin.

The sin argument also forms the starting point for Francis Spufford in his fascinating book *Unapologetic*, which he subtitles *Why, despite everything, Christianity can still make surprisingly emotional sense.* Not that he calls it sin. He has a much more colourful version: HPtFtU – the human propensity to fuck things up. For him the way forward 'begins with the admission that you really are guilty of the particular bit of HPtFtU which is making you feel like shit. If you don't give the weight in your chest its true name you can't even begin. It's guilt that drags at your steps, it's guilt that paints your mornings black.'[6] It's hard to disagree that this is a universal human experience, but I don't see why it requires a religious answer of divine forgiveness rather than an everyday recourse to therapy and asking forgiveness from those we have offended.

The other foundation stone of Christian theology has been the authority of the Church. The early Church is supposed to have established the truth of the key Christian doctrines at a series of councils of bishops, protected from error by the Holy Spirit. These councils passed from age to age what was called 'the deposit of faith' – the core of doctrinal beliefs that still forms the basis of the creed recited in so many churches today. For example, many congregations are invited to declare every Sunday that we believe the Holy Spirit 'proceeds from the Father and the Son [*Filioque*]'. Unless, that is, we are in an Eastern Orthodox church, in which case the Holy Spirit proceeds only from the Father. A rather specialized metaphysical difference, you might think, and one that would be impossible to resolve either way. And yet it was this one word, *Filioque*, that was the cause of the total schism between the Roman and Eastern Churches that has continued to the present day. Even if we weren't worried about such abstruse relationships between members of the Trinity, such complete contradictions between Churches that claim to proclaiming God's own truths don't offer grounds for confidence in the Church as the guardian of all truth.

The matter became worse in the Roman Catholic Church when in the nineteenth century the Vatican Council (again under the supposed guidance of God) proclaimed that the decisions of the Pope taken *ex cathedra* are infallible. Today Canon Law (749.1) declares that by virtue of his office, the Supreme Pontiff teaches infallibly when he proclaims by a definitive act a doctrine to be held concerning faith or morals.

Once again, this offers a useful shortcut to the truth, since God Himself is apparently speaking through the Pope. Unfortunately, to accept this idea you would have to accept the things that God has apparently said through this mouthpiece: like the entirely new doctrine announced by Pope Pius XII as recently as 1950 that Jesus' mother Mary was carried up to heaven bodily at the end of her life. And as to the rules on morality, taught as equally infallible, you would have to accept that God had absolutely prohibited contraception. Worse still, your confidence in the divine authority of the Church will be shaken when the Protestant Church declares that God takes an opposite view on contraception, and goes on to state in its Westminster Confession of Faith that: 'The Pope of Rome… is that Antichrist, that man of sin, and son of perdition, that exalts himself, in the Church, against Christ and all that is called God.'[7]

When the psalmist sang 'put not your trust in princes,' he should perhaps have added, 'especially not in the princes of the church.'

A different approach is to see the traditional, supernatural claims of Christianity as ways of dressing up everyday truths about our common experience of being human. This produces a form of secularized theology of the kind powerfully proposed in the later books of the Cambridge radical theologian Don Cupitt. In this way, talk about God becomes no more than talk about the highest human aspirations, and Christianity is ultimately a system of ethics.

While this can make Christianity more easily acceptable to today's humanists, it is not clear to me that this hollowed-out version of religion has anything distinctive to offer. It feels like a different way of describing the ultimate meaninglessness of life, dressed up in highfalutin' language. To quote the Austrian sociologist Peter Berger:

> A secularized Christianity... has to go to considerable exertion to demonstrate that the religious label, as modified in conformity with the spirit of the age, has anything special to offer. Why should one buy psychotherapy or racial liberalism in a 'Christian' package, when the same commodities are available under purely secular... labels? The preference for the former will probably be limited to people with a sentimental nostalgia for traditional symbols.[8]

But, as I hinted at the previous chapter, I am equally unpersuaded by the non-religious responses to our question: What is the meaning of life? Is it all for nothing? For the existentialists the answer is: Yes, it is all for nothing – get over it. For Camus an individual overcomes the ultimate absurdity of life through their free commitment to important work. His position relies on the crucial idea of human freedom: the power to exercise our free will to choose the form of existence we want to live. But isn't this itself a problem for such a secularist, scientific world view? As we shall see in a later chapter, science has no obvious place for human freedom. On the contrary, it posits a deterministic world of cause and effect where my every decision is fully determined by the preceding state of my body and brain. I may think I am freely deciding, but either that is an illusion, or the scientific laws of cause and effect no longer hold. So, responding to the absurdity of life with what secular science sees as the absurd illusion of freedom seems self-defeating.

But I suspect that for many people the answer is much simpler. Just carry on *as if* life had a meaning, pretending that life has an ultimate purpose in spite of the evidence to the contrary. The only way to cope is just to get on with everyday life. Leave the big questions to others. Best not dwell on things. Above all, don't think about death. But the limits of this approach of avoidance can come home to us from time to time, for example, when the children start asking difficult questions like, 'Are you going to die, Mummy? Am I going to die?'

Peter Berger in his book *A Rumour of Angels* points to the comfort and reassurance that every mother will naturally offer to her child, frightened in the night: 'Don't be afraid – everything is in order, everything is alright.' But, says Berger, secular science responds that she's whistling in the dark. Ultimately, it's not all going to be alright. 'She is lying, out of love to be sure… but lying all the same. Why? Because the reassurance… implies a statement about reality as such. And that reality is only genuinely reassuring if there is some truth in the religious interpretation of human existence.'[9]

So, I have to conclude that none of these starting points work for me as paths to faith.

The Construction of Religious Meaning

Religion is an attempt to construct meaning
in the face of the relentless pain and injustice of life.[1]
Karen Armstrong

I give the name 'God' to the unknown dimension that underlies the meaning of everything. Not a first cause, like the traditional arguments for God, but the ultimate meaning. And to underpin that meaning of everything, this God must be *real* – must be more than the *idea* of ultimate meaning.

This God is 'something more': something more than the world we can observe, something more than the ideas in our heads. That is as far as I am prepared to claim about the God I believe in. What that Something More could be takes us into the realm of imaginative invention and metaphor. Traditional theology calls this the negative way, 'the way of unknowing'. Thomas Aquinas, often described as the greatest theologian, having written more than 2,000 pages about God, finally burned them, saying: 'We cannot know what God is, only what He is not.'

If I needed a text from the New Testament, I could quote St Paul. In speaking about 'faith' (using the same Greek word we translated earlier as 'belief'), he says: 'Faith is the substance of things hoped for, the evidence of things not seen.'[2]

This is not a proof. It's not something I know. It's something I choose to believe. It is the substance of what I hope for. It is not based on any evidence 'seen' – any empirical evidence. Yes, Freud, I *want* to believe it because it explains why my life has meaning, but I have taken that step consciously, and not as a frightened child longing for the comfort of a heavenly father. Yes, Marx, this could be seen as opium for the masses, but does it have to be? The best examples of Christian lives are of struggle and self-sacrifice, more than of drugged comfort and luxurious ease.

Moreover, my need for meaning is a real need, not to be dismissed. The fact that I feel a need for water shouldn't stop me from drinking. On the contrary. Certainly, in Freud's view, it should stop me being satisfied by drinking imaginary water. But what to do in a situation when I have no way of knowing for sure either way what is truth and what is illusion? If we are in danger of dying in an endless desert and think we see an oasis, doesn't it make sense to head for it – even if it may turn out to be a mirage? The alternative is definitely dying of thirst – of dying, by analogy, of a meaningless life.

This is all beginning to sound like Blaise Pascal's wager – our bet on God – our guess about what provides life with the underpinning of the meaning we experience. But we have to adapt Pascal's famous wager a bit. As he presents it, the wager is this: either God exists or He doesn't. If we bet that He doesn't exist, then we don't have to stake much in this life, but if we lose the bet, we are sentenced to eternal damnation. Whereas if we bet that God does exist, then our stake is very high (a life of self-denial), but we could win everlasting felicity in heaven. So, it comes down to a choice between more happiness now or more happiness after death.

Put like that, it raises the obvious objection that, far from being a no-brain bet, I could be throwing away the chance of happiness in this life for the unknown possibility of happiness in the next. Indeed, it is only the horror of losing the bet – Hell – that makes this dilemma at all urgent.

So I see the wager a little differently – and in terms of life both now and in the future. In my version, if I am wrong in betting on God, then I am living a life that is only imaginary in its ultimate meaningfulness, and after death there turns out to be nothing. Whereas if I am right in putting my money on God, then I have a meaningful life now and at least the possibility of some kind of heaven thereafter. That seems like a much better bet.

This is also my response to the famous advertisement for atheism on London buses: 'There's probably no God. Now stop worrying and enjoy your life.' My response is: 'Yes, there may or may not be a God, but I enjoy life more, not less, in the belief that there is.'

But this does raise another problem. If belief costs me so little (at most opening me to ridicule and wasting some time in church when I could be in the pub or playing with the kids), then is such cheap, easy-come-easy-go belief real at all? It could be one of those claims that, as Wittgenstein says, make no difference to anything in the real world, like a gear wheel that turns without any connection to the rest of the machine.[3]

So, let's apply the test of this religious belief that is proposed on the side of the bus: whether it results in a person who lives a life that is meaningful and purposeful in the ordinary sense of those words, a life that is happy, fulfilling, and fruitful to others. As Jesus would say, like trees we are judged by the fruit we bear, the fruitfulness of our lives. By that test I would claim Christian agnosticism passes.

But what if we lose our bet on God and it was all an illusion? Well, the fulfilled life was real – and that after all was the very thing Jesus is said to have promised: life in all its fullness. It's a bit like the current joke: 'What if climate change is an illusion and we've created a better world for nothing?'

All this is nothing to do with discredited arguments from Creationism or Intelligent Design. It is not an attempt to persuade you that God exists. Rather I am explaining how I have come to believe what I do. It starts as a response to the question 'Is this all there is?' To which my response is 'No, it can't be.' It's as simple as that – an emotional response, a feeling. But then it forms itself into an argument of sorts. If this were all there was, then how could my life have the meaning it does? But I feel my life does have ultimate meaning, therefore in my picture of the world – a picture I make up – this passing world cannot be all there is. And the Something More I call God.

Alongside the constant question 'Is this all there is?' comes the accompanying question 'Is everything for nothing?' Are all the wonderful things and loved people in my life going to be lost? If they are going to be lost, then how I behave towards them, while most important for now, doesn't ultimately matter as much. And yet I feel the opposite. I feel it matters profoundly what I do. I feel that the things I and others do are not lost in empty space – 'not even a smile is lost', as Pierre Teillard de Chardin says in *Le Milieu Divin*.[4] By the way, be warned. I'm going to be referring to this quotation many times before we're finished.

So, you can see my train of thought: if there is to be meaning that lasts, then I must be part of a meaningful universe that has some underlying purpose. And so, I start thinking in phrases like 'nothing is lost', 'life after death', 'being held', 'a caring God'.

So far, then, I am an agnostic who believes in a God who gives my life and everyone's life ultimate meaning. After that, everything is invention. Everything we grandly call Theology is a way of arranging tentative Lego bricks of metaphor onto this foundation of meaning, of a belief that 'This is not all there is'.

And for these shaky buildings not to fall over, the test is not 'Are these additional beliefs proved by evidence to be true?' but rather 'Are these beliefs internally consistent?' So, for example, we might start by linking this mysterious God of whom we *know* nothing to something we do experience as the highest value in the meaning we experience in our lives – love. So might venture: 'God is love'. And then extend that to: 'Ubi caritas Deus ibi est' – wherever there is love, God is there. We'll come back to this.

As we start to think speculatively about what this unknowable God could be like, searching for a Theology that is coherent, inconsistencies and contradictions can be thrown up. So, for example, if we are looking for part of our Lego construction to account for the fact of evil and the idea of justice, we might come up with the metaphor of place called Hell to which evil people are consigned. But that then raises questions like: 'How could a loving God consign anyone to everlasting torment in Hell?' That would be incoherent. So we have to abandon the idea of Hell and build a different model. And so Theology proceeds. But we shouldn't imagine that our Lego towers correspond to how things actually are in some knowable, metaphysical world.

The original title of this book was *Make-Believe*. This was an allusion to the old 1930s song *It's only a Paper Moon*. I'd quote the song here if I could. But when I checked the copyright position for including the first four lines of the song, I was told it would cost $1,000 to quote those lines, and that was for only five years. So instead of quoting the song, I will have to go the roundabout route of telling you in prose form that what it says is that it's only a paper moon that's shining over a cardboard sea, but that this would be more than make-believe if you were to believe in me.

Perhaps this song helps me explain what I mean by claiming that religion is a totally human creation and that all our language about God is poetry. The picture we create of God can only be a paper moon: a human picture of a dimension which, if it exists, we can never define or pin down with evidence. And the grand dioceses of the Church are no more than cardboard sees: flimsy institutions we have constructed that can never be the source of infallible truth. But the song, like these thoughts, is about love not astronomical science: it's about believing in more than believing that. That's why 'it wouldn't be make-believe, if I believed in God.'

The Strange Phenomenon of Free Will

Man is a masterpiece of creation if for no other reason than that, all the weight of evidence for determinism notwithstanding, he believes he has free will.[1]
Georg Christoph Lichtenberg

I've said that I'm basing my belief in God on a feeling. I can't believe that my life and everyone else's lives have no meaning. Without a sense of ultimate meaning, so much of what I put effort into doing would not seem worth doing. But there's another very powerful factor that weighs with me: another strong feeling that needs a context to explain it. And that is my strong belief that, in spite of the evidence, I have free will. I can decide how to live my life, what my goals are to be, how I can play a part in creating a better world. My choices are not for nothing. As before, without this belief it would be hard to see how my life means anything.

The problem is that, in a secular universe as described by science, it looks impossible to have free will. It's a world purely of cause and effect. Everything that happens is 100 per cent determined by what happened before. If you knew the exact state of my body and brain at time x, and you knew every detail of how the rules of physics and the other sciences operate, then you could predict exactly what I would do next, at time y. You could predict what I would think, what I would choose, what I would do – and even what reasons I would give for why I did it, and why I would think, wrongly, that I had free will. This is predestination quite as harsh as the strictest Calvinists would have it.

Nor does the randomness of quantum physics help. Suppose the choice I made wasn't entirely determined but came about because of a random fluctuation in my brain. That hardly convinces me that it was my own, free choice, for which I am content to be morally praised or blamed. No, it was an accident, not something I chose.

And yet don't we all work on the assumption that we are freely choosing our life path, and that our societies can choose the future they want? Indeed, our way of running society depends on it. No choice, no blame. Actions are wrong, in the words of the Prayer Book, when they are done 'through our own deliberate fault'. This makes no sense if science makes determinism unavoidable. Nothing I do is morally wrong, because I could not have done otherwise. In that case, my sense that I have free will is an illusion, and morality as commonly understood is meaningless. Shoshana Zuboff, the American academic and author put it very well in a recent podcast. 'The very prospect of a democratic society is impossible to imagine without the idea that we, as individuals, as citizens, have the capacity to choose our actions and to fulfil our vision of the future.'[2]

So, we are in the same bind as we were with the meaning of life. We feel we are free to decide things. Secular science says we can't be. So we need another explanation or hypothesis about how the freedom we experience could be real. This is not a question of believing impossible things for the sake of it, but believing hypotheses that we can't prove but that make sense of the basis on which we operate in everyday life. Since there must be free will to give my life any meaning, then the universe cannot be the deterministic, meaningless arena of the non-believer. Somehow something else is going on that is bigger and beyond and as we don't know what it is, let's call it God, Horatio.

Of course I haven't solved the age-old philosophical problem of the freedom of the will. Bringing God into the equation doesn't solve it in its own terms. I still can't claim to understand how free choice can operate in the world of physics. Rather I am arguing the other way round. Since I experience my own free will, and since my moral universe depends on free will, then we need the bigger picture: the inclusion of something beyond the world of everyday physics.

So, is everything that follows more make-believe? Yes. It is an attempt to construct a picture of how the world works that fits with the meaning I need to feel it has. I am simply laying out a worldview that makes sense for me – and makes sense of my life. Suddenly this make-believe that I'm spinning here seems very insubstantial. Why should you, grandchildren, be remotely interested in this worldview if it's simply what I've made up? Because, in the first place, what is made up is only the *picture*, not the underlying potential *reality* that it is picturing. And that could be the most important dimension of reality that there is. And secondly because the pictures here have mostly not been created by me. As I go on in later chapters to sketch in colours and shapes to the picture I'm painting, I will be looking for help. Although I don't want to revert to relying on the past for authority, I will be grateful as I stumble forward for those ideas, glimpses and metaphors from the past that can resonate with the twenty-first-century world we now inhabit.

A few years ago when I was on my own on Patmos (having gone back, as I mentioned, to this 'holy island' after exactly 50 years, as a retreat and small pilgrimage), I experienced something of this connection to the past. The early morning liturgy in the tiny convent church really connected with something deep within me. The chanting of the priest – some words redolent, some mysterious – the singing of the nuns, the young mothers bringing tiny children forward to kiss the icons, the old fishermen crossing themselves, the sense of time standing still, sharing a liturgy that had continued virtually unchanged for close on two thousand years... It gave me a sense in this darkened, cave-like church of an initiation as old as the Eleusinian mysteries, where people experience not new knowledge but personal transformation. All this was happening to me without any rational explanation, but with an undeniable feeling of being held and enriched by the experience of being here, today, for these two hours.

Experiencing something beyond my make-believe. Something unknowable but something internally tangible.

Then a few weeks later I had a dream. A friend was setting us a puzzle: a mystery in six parts that he wanted us to help him solve. After a while we solved the first section. That led on to the second, which we also worked out together. But at stage three and beyond, we were stuck. We couldn't work it out at all. Then my friend explained to us that it was this part of the puzzle, steps 3, 4, 5 and 6, that he was desperate for our help to solve. To that end he had invented steps 1 and 2 himself, thinking that because we knew him and the way he thought, we would be able to solve them, and that this would give us a run-up to the real mysteries that he hadn't invented and wanted to solve.

That seemed a helpful dream: my unconscious reminding me that although I am here making up a set of beliefs as a way of underpinning the meaning of the world as I experience it, those beliefs in turn imply a whole realm of unknowable reality – what Paul Tillich called 'the ground of being'; what Jung hoped to tap into as 'the collective unconscious'. If there is something of the kind I am guessing at, then it can't be a small something. If it is to fulfil the function of underpinning everything, it must be the most important something there is. And this is what I am so grateful to catch a glimpse of in those moments in church (in so few churches, sadly), in the woods, in the concert hall – above all, in the dark.

I had an extraordinary experience in Seoul. My wife Anuradha and I went into an installation in a downtown office building called *Dialogue in the Dark,* where we were invited to experience a world of complete darkness. Watches and phones – anything that might give light – had to be left outside the door of the room. It was distinctly alarming as well as disorientating. Then we were guided forward by a person who introduced himself with the unusual nickname of 'Handsome'. He described where we were, as we walked through what we experienced as woodland, into a market, onto a boat – with the sounds, smells and the objects our hands and feet encountered creating a vivid world in the blackness.

As our journey came to an end, I asked our guide how he had learned his own way around – had he practised with the lights on? 'No need,' he said. 'I'm blind.'

A sudden revelation in so many ways: that this world of darkness that was so unfamiliar to us he lived all the time; that in this total darkness he was the guide we could not do without; that he was handsome without ever having seen himself. And that this is how I stumble through this darkly mysterious life. I know we are making up pictures of cosmic, heavenly kingdoms that we cannot see. But I have experienced the supporting hands of the guides – living and dead – who have held my hand and given me confidence that as I stumble forward, I will not fall.

Which Takes Us to Life after Death

What here is faithfully begun
Will be completed, not undone.[1]
Arthur Hugh Clough

When my father died, alongside the piercing grief was the sense of 'What a waste!' His years of detailed study, decades of high-level experience of government, poems written and poems unwritten, memories never shared… Could all these just be thrown into the crematorium oven as if they had never been added to the sum of what this world means? If the world means anything, and of course I believe it does, then it makes no sense for all this to be thrown away.

And at scale, what is the sense of creating societies and whole civilisations that we know will eventually be destroyed, if not by our global warming then by the ineluctable power of the laws of entropy by which all physical reality will end in chaos? It may provide bittersweet feelings in existential poets that nothing lasts, but to me it means that nothing is ultimately worth doing. Rather, I take as central to any meaningful universe – to any picture of the purposes of God – that it is not for nothing. That is the refrain of Pierre Teilhard de Chardin that I keep coming back to: nothing is lost: not a smile, not a good action done in secret, not the lifetime of my father, my daughter Boo, or myself.

Here is Teilhard's full quote:

> A thought, a material improvement, a harmony, a unique nuance of human love, the enchanting complexity of a smile or a glance, all these new beauties that appear for the first time, in me or around me, on the human face of the earth – I cherish them like children and cannot believe that they will die entirely in their

> flesh. If I believed that these things were to perish for ever, should I have given them life? Show all your faithful, Lord, in what a full and true sense 'their work follows them into your kingdom.'... Little by little, stage by stage, everything is finally linked to the extreme centre in quo omnia constant (in Whom all things hold together).[2]

So although I can add little so far to my picture of this God I am guessing at – this meaningful universe I am believing in – I certainly need to add this: that life and love are not wiped out by death. If that were so, then this meaning itself would turn into meaninglessness.

Indeed, I don't think this is just me. I see this as the assumption, sometimes unconscious, which alone gives meaning to the everyday life of many of us. As Dostoyevsky puts in the mouth of Ivan Fyodorovitch Karamazov: 'If you were to destroy in mankind the belief in immortality, not only love but every living force maintaining the life of the world would at once be dried up.'[3]

My favourite Archbishop of Canterbury, Robert Runcie, whom I filmed for a year all over the world, put it in strikingly similar terms in conversation with the writer John Mortimer:

> I can't believe, when I see the promise of Christ expressed in a particular person, that that's all coming to an end. But as for the geography and climate of the after-life, well, I'm an agnostic about that.[4]

Now, although I am not suggesting that I have any evidence for life after death, if I am to believe in it, then I do need to show that the concept is possible – that it's not logically incoherent. The coherence of the notion of immortality would typically be attacked as follows. We know at least that a body does not survive death. Moreover, we can no longer separate the person from the body, as a doctrine of the soul might try to do. Memory is tied directly to the brain cells, and personality to (among other things) the endocrine system. Therefore if the body does not survive, the person cannot survive.

I attempted to answer this challenge in a paper I wrote as a student in 1966. I still find it plausible, so I will simply quote it here:

> I do not think that we can save the doctrine of life after death by any definition of 'person' that does not involve the body. Nor need we, since the church has always preached not the immortality of the soul, but the resurrection of the body. May I try to make sense of this notion in modern terms by indulging in some theological science fiction? We can do without something like this, but only if we are prepared to put sufficient weight on 'resurrection': if we are prepared to believe that God can and will reanimate particular matter: I find this implausible, however, and thus feel justified in trying to give some sense to St Paul's picture of a *spiritual* body. I wish to suggest that though we have no reason to believe that the matter of my body will survive death, we have no reason to believe that the body itself will not.
>
> We must start with the philosophical commonplace that I am the same person as I was 20 years ago, although almost no actual cells have survived from that body to this. But more than that, I want to say that I have the same body now as I had then. If this is granted, then one must conclude that the individuating characteristic is not the material but the pattern. As Pat Boone used to sing: 'Your separate parts are not unknown, but the way you assemble them's all your own.' This is clear from the way that new materials are continuously built into the body by the DNA and RNA. At this level *pattern*

means exactly *information*. A person is created initially on the basis of a set of pure information, and his body remains the same body because, on the whole, material is replaced according to the pattern specified by this information. Of course, a person is more that the sum of the information written on his or her DNA, but is this additional element non-informational? Many philosophers point to memories as the basis of the continuity of personality and memories clearly consist of pure information. The point here again will be that the information itself could survive the material on which it is stored, the brain cells.

I have started with the two simplest cases, where the description of the part of the 'body' is actually stored in the body in the form of pure information. But for the rest – the particular form of the mature body, inasfar as this is thought relevant to personality, essential self, etc., surely this is open to complete description; and in particular there is no special feature which puts such a description beyond the scope of the omniscience of God.

Now for the jump. I want to say that it is this pattern of information that forms the essence of the individual body, and thus of the individual person. We know that the matter of the body does not survive in its characteristic form, but it remains a possibility that the distinctive *pattern* of the body could survive, either embodied in entirely new material ('sown perishable and raised imperishable' to quote St Paul again), or else simply as pure information (for example, on tape).

There is clearly nothing to entail this survival (though the genetic transfer of information is suggestive), but this is the other side of the Church's teaching: that God must be trusted

> to maintain this continuity. Thus we come to a sort of Middle Platonism: there exists in contrast to this knockabout self a pure 'ideal' self, which exists as a thought in the mind of God. Faith in life after death is, then, faith that God can hold us in life by His total knowledge of us – in whose book are all our members written.
>
> The great problem with all this is that of the identity of indiscernibles. Could any copy of me, however exact, become me? Or if a copy could, could a description? For one thing, the destruction of the original seems incidental. In that case there would be two of me, and which would be the real me? But the key thought experiment is this. **Draw a line: how can anything you may create on the other side make my consciousness cross the line?**
>
> Since this is in no sense a philosophical treatment of this problem, but merely speculation about possibilities, I do not want to guess at the philosophical results in this field. I would only say – we know that a person can survive the almost total change from child to old man; is it impossible that he should survive this other change? Also, since the step is from time into eternity, the simple logic of temporal continuity may break down. On the positive side, this picture may be thought to derive support from, and also itself to illuminate, the Christian view that the moment of passing from death to life is not the moment of physical death, but the moment of salvation (which in these terms would come out as incorporation into the eternal divine life).

If you have agreed so far, you will probably reply – but that's just what I mean by the soul! (See Wittgenstein Philosophical Investigations II, iv)

That's what I wrote 50 years ago and it still seems to me to make sense. Indeed, there has recently been an upsurge of interest in Ray Kurzweil's ideas along similar lines. Even the Guardian newspaper could, without apparent embarrassment on behalf of its rationalist readers, print the headline: 'Immortality Will Be Delivered by the Singularity Say Scientists.' As Kurzweil puts it: 'With nanotechnology, we will be able to go beyond the limits of biology, and replace your current human body version 1.0 with a dramatically upgraded version 2.0, providing radical life extension.' That sounds like something close to my idea of the 'spiritual body'. Then the argument continues in a similar way to my old ideas, except now with memory chips instead of tape. These scientists believe that:

> We will achieve 'virtual immortality,' when the fullness of our mental selves can be uploaded perfectly to non-biological media (such as silicon chips), and our mental selves will live on beyond the demise of our fleshy, physical bodies.[5]

So far so good. However, this still depends on the possibility that my consciousness can 'cross the line' – the imaginary chalk line in my original thought-experiment drawn between my body as it is now and the perfect copy standing on the other side of the line. If my consciousness can't somehow cross that line, then, when I die, my consciousness dies too. That is why my model relies on the guess that my survival relies on the power of God, in whose infinite and eternal mind I am held in existence. The simplest analogy here is the digital cloud. My computer's information is safe because it is held in the cloud. Jesus ascends after death into the clouds in his spiritual body. I am held in the cloud of God's love. All pictures, but are they pictures of logical impossibilities or helpful ways of understanding what may be the ultimate mysteries of the universe?

Therefore, rather than the singularity, I am happy with St Paul's notion of the spiritual body. There's a wonderful image for this, which my wife Anuradha has just written. It's in a different, fictional context, but I hope she doesn't mind my adopting it as a brilliant image of the transition through death to a spiritual body:

> I've just heard the most hair-raising thing on the radio about caterpillars. When they get into their cocoons, they allow their cells to melt so they can be re-formed into butterfly cells.
>
> It's incredible. How could you possibly let your caterpillar self die – just because of some promise, some vague hope, that if you could only let go your old self, you would come back as a more brilliant self than before? How could you be that trusting?
>
> I can't imagine ever having the courage even to start the process by entering a dark tunnel, the cocoon, and staying there, melting... Sacrificing my old self, trusting life that I really will come out one day as a butterfly. It would be terrifyingly risky. Too much for me.
>
> And imagine the shock of finding yourself reborn with wings! Waking up in the morning to feel your shoulder blades odd and heavy, and then find the back of your pyjama top filled with something strange, delicate, but huge and folded up, like waking up and finding you're an angel.

From pictures of an individual's spiritual body we move to pictures of heaven. The traditional Christian heaven is not in good shape. Preachers tell us lamely that they do not believe that heaven is a literal world of harps and clouds: rather it is the state of being in the presence of God. They destroy the only image we had, an image they were happy enough to inculcate in us in the hymns and stories of Sunday school, and they offer us in its place an abstraction. So, either heaven drops out of Christian imagination, or we need new pictures of it. Personally, I like the idea behind *Resurrection*, a popular song of the '60s by the Belgian nun Soeur Sourire, which pictures heaven as a party – the kind of party to which we all dream of being invited:

> Velasquez et Michelange de loin se reconnaitront
> Et plein d'une joie sans mélange,
> Designant l'homme du Cromagnon.
> Pour accomplir leur béat et nourir les affamés
> Les petits scouts de l'Alaska vendront des chocolats glacés.
>
> Le bienheureux Dominique et Saint Francois retrouvés,
> Boirant la Benedictine pour féter leur amitié.[6]

The advantage of imagery that is light and occasionally ludicrous is that it does not take itself so seriously, it risks being taken literally. Nevertheless, the understanding behind this song does convey to me something true and important about heaven, something that Teillard de Chardin (yes, I am going to quote it again) puts like this:

> A thought, a material improvement, a harmony, a unique nuance of human love, the enchanting complexity of a smile or a glance, all these new beauties that appear for the first time, in me or around me, on the human face of the earth – I cherish them like children and cannot believe that they will die entirely in their flesh. If I believed that these things were to perish for ever, should I have given them life?... Show all your faithful, Lord, in what a full and true sense 'their work follows them into your kingdom'... Little by little, stage by stage, everything is finally linked to the extreme centre in quo omnia constant.[7]

Teillard de Chardin was himself an outstanding example of a theologian with the courage to mint new religious language, drawn in his case from the secular vocabularies of human and cosmic evolutionary theory.

In conclusion, I don't *know* that there is life after death. There is no evidence for it that I can see. I *believe* that there is life after death because without it the strong feeling I have that life is meaningful would not make sense. Moreover, I think I have shown that the idea of life after death is not logically impossible.

I love the lines of the Victorian poet Arthur Hugh Clough:

Ah yet, when all is thought and said,
The heart still overrules the head;
Still what we hope we must believe,
And what is given us receive;

Must still believe, for still we hope
That in a world of larger scope,
What here is faithfully begun
Will be completed, not undone.[8]

Now that I am clear that I believe in life after death, a lot of other things follow.

The Great All or Nothing

The greatness of something incomprehensible but all-present.[1]
Leo Tolstoy

When Prince Andrew, in Tolstoy's *War and Peace*, is lying left for dead on the battlefield, he sees life with a sudden clarity.

> 'It would be good,' thought Prince Andrew, glancing at the icon his sister had hung around his neck with such emotion and reverence, 'it would be good if everything were as clear and simple as it seems to Mary. How good it would be to know where to seek for help in this life, and what to expect after it beyond the grave! How happy and calm I should be if I could now say: "Lord, have mercy on me!"... But to whom should I say that? Either to a Power indefinable, incomprehensible, which I not only cannot address but which I cannot even express in words – the Great All or Nothing,' said he to himself, 'or to that God who has been sewn into this amulet by Mary! There is nothing certain, nothing at all except the unimportance of everything I understand, and the greatness of something incomprehensible but all-present.'[1]

Though I have this chapter ahead of me, there is really nothing I can add to Tolstoy. I need God to underpin the meaning to my life that I experience. If I am to go beyond this and make some connection with this God who is ultimately unknowable – 'the Great All or Nothing' – then I'm going to need some icon like Mary's. A picture that stands for something invisible. The alternative is to stop with a kind of deism (the idea that there is a power behind the world that has no connection with it). But the kind of meaning and help for life that I am feeling the need of requires some kind of connection – what has traditionally been called a personal God.

Unfortunately, to fill out my picture of the Great All or Nothing, the simplest, traditional avenue is not available to me. In classic Christianity, all questions can be answered by the idea of revelation. This revelation can be accessed by reading the Bible (or other sacred works) as the direct words of God. I can't imagine many people could accept this any more than I could. The Bible is all too human, with as many outworn and contradictory ideas as it has spiritual insights.

I start instead with my central question: What cosmic framework must there be to underpin life's meaning? It follows that the nature of that framework must fit the meaning I experience. If, for example, love is central to my sense of the meaning of my life, then my picture cannot be of an uncaring God. My picture of God reflects my *values*. If I think forgiveness is a value that inspires me and works for me in daily life, then I picture a forgiving God: a God of grace. Conversely if I were to think that just vengeance is an important virtue, then I could easily come to believe in a vengeful God, defending the oppressed and punishing the wicked. Of course, I go for the former.

Thus, my picture of the unknowable God takes on the colours of my values. My progression of thought goes like this. For me love is my highest value. It would make no sense if acts of love, particularly sacrificial acts of love, were not central to my sense of ultimate meaning. Loving actions and loved people must not be lost. Therefore heaven must be a place of love, and cannot at the same time be a place of the opposite. So, God is loving. Indeed, God *is* love. Indeed, where love is, there God is. Just as God is the ground of being, so God is the ground of love – God underpins love, guarantees that it is not for nothing. 'No one has ever seen God. If we love one another, God dwells in us.'[2]

But of course this does not mean that love will always win out in the here and now. That would take us back to the interfering, judgemental God. Nor does it take us to the most common misrepresentation of Christianity and many religions: 'If you are good, you'll go to heaven' – usually applied in judgement of other people. Rather, my picture of heaven follows from the belief that the qualities and people I value aren't a flash in the cosmic pan but will not be lost: they will be safe in the mind of God or held in the arms of God. And this gets us into parental metaphors – God as father or mother. This in no longer just believing *that* (that God exists), but believing *in* (trusting my life to God).

My picture of God is a jigsaw. With jigsaws I start with the corners, then fit the straight edges, then the rest. So far, I have, I hope, put in place my corner pieces of belief: things that I definitely believe in and which underpin my view of the meaning of life. Then I have worked along the edges with additional pieces that fit together, arguing for their cogency and looking for an overall pattern. I could leave it there, but it would be a mental skeleton. So I begin to fill in the picture with scores of jigsaw pieces from traditional Christian ideas and metaphors. I don't agree with most of them taken literally, but I love many of them poetically. Moreover, this allows me to connect to the pictures created by the Christian poets, composers and painters in whose work I can therefore immerse myself. So, for example, I can be moved and uplifted by Kathleen Ferrier singing 'I know that my Redeemer liveth, and that He shall stand at the latter day upon the earth.' Not something I believe literally, but wonderful poetry from the Book of Job set to wonderful music by Handel. And more than that, it evokes a religious response that simply would not be there if I did not have the corner-stone belief that we have a divine destiny that transcends death.

And moving a little nearer our own times, think of the poets around the late nineteenth and early twentieth centuries. This was the period of the ending of Victorian religious certainties, yet listening the other day to a BBC programme about the poets that broke the old poetic mould – Eliot, Auden, Manley

Hopkins, Sitwell – it suddenly struck me that they were all not just Christian by vague association but by active choice. As poets that's where their imaginative, intuitional search for meaning took them, even though, for example, the reaction of the literary establishment to the news of Eliot's joining the Church of England was straightforwardly dismissive. Virginia Woolf wrote: 'Poor dear Tom Eliot… may be called dead to us all from this day forward. There's something obscene in a living person sitting by the fire and believing in God.'[3] But of course my suggestion here too is the wrong way round – I follow the people whose values I share, rather than adopting the values and religious language of those whose artistry I admire, still less those whose celebrity is established. Celebrity endorsement of particular religions is for the birds.

This focus on metaphors requires a further step in my thinking. If we can only speak about God through metaphors, which metaphors should I use? If we can only imagine God through pictures that we draw ourselves, which pictures make most sense to me? The simple answer is that it makes sense to adopt the imagery of the religious cultures in which I have been brought up and in which I now live. Then I can relate directly to the art I see around me, the religious music I hear and even the church services I take part in. But within this tradition there are still important choices to be make. I could, for example, adopt the imagery of the Old Testament. Then I would see God as Isaiah did – sitting upon a throne, high and lifted up, above him the winged seraphim, calling through the smoke: 'Holy, holy, holy is the Lord of armies.'

There was a powerful example of this kind of Old Testament picture of God still being offered to us today when I was in church in Mezzolombardo, a small town in the foothills of the mountains of Northern Italy. It was a Catholic church, but the reading would have been prescribed this Sunday in many denominations around the world. For me there was a real shock in the juxtaposition that followed. First the reading of the story of the people of Israel under Moses and Joshua fighting to seize the land promised to them by God from the indigenous Amalcites. The reading ended: 'So Joshua defeated Amalek and his people, passing them by the edge of the sword.'[4] And then these words were immediately followed by: '*Parola di Dio. Rendiamo grazie a Dio.*' ('This is the word of God. Let us give thanks to God.') I don't think so! I don't think those are the words of God and I don't think we would thank Him if they were.

There are many such pictures of God that I could never take to heart: the Sky Father jealous of rival gods, the god who will only forgive us if his son is killed, the god who demands his followers to live by despotic rules, the god who can't get enough praise from his kneeling courtiers, the god who will save my friends at the expense of my enemies, the god who will damn to eternal torment those who don't believe in him, the god of battles in whose sign we can conquer, the god whose existence we can prove, the god who has established the church as the only path to salvation. If that is the only god on offer, I would not only deny him, I would join my atheist friends in denouncing him as a tyrant of the very worst sort.

What makes sense to me is the picture of God that Jesus taught: the unknown God in the image of a heavenly father. OK, Freud, I know my own father was away from home far too much. OK, Germaine, I know father includes mother. All metaphors are limited, but this one resonates strongly with me.

If Jesus prays to 'Our Father which art in heaven', then the striking implication is that Jesus is not a son of God any more – or less – than we all are. It speaks immediately to the spark of divinity in each of us. It invites us to celebrate that in ourselves and to recognize it in everyone else. As such, it's an image worth cherishing and a prayer worth praying.

If Jesus says, 'Blessed are the poor for theirs is the kingdom of heaven,'[5] that implies a striking reversal of the usual priorities for our picture of God or the way we run our societies.

If the gospel-writer John half-remembers or imagines Jesus saying, 'In my Father's house are many mansions... I go to prepare a place for you,'[6] then there's a picture of life after death that I, like so many, find profoundly helpful when we mourn.

In this way, my pictures of the divine are forming patterns that help shape my life, not because I know that they are accurate reflections of a metaphysical reality, but because they fit into the patterns of my life's meaning, as I struggle to learn how best to live.

If picturing God and other religious realities is a challenge for all of us, then it is even more so for filmmakers. In my years working for BBC religious television, I faced this challenge every day. The ways I reflected on it at the time might be helpful here.

It is one of the most familiar clichés of any discussion of television that it is an entirely inappropriate medium for the communication of ideas. Television is good at places and people, it is said, not abstract ideas. So when they knew where I worked, friends used to commiserate with me for having the doubly impossible task of trying to communicate not only ideas, but ideas about that most abstract of all subjects, Theology. To film religious places and religious people seems feasible enough, but how does one explore on television whether the ideas that motivate such people are believable, without turning to that television form of last resort, the talking head?

I found then and I find now the search for contemporary images for religious ideas and ideals by far the most satisfying aspect of my work as a filmmaker. To find such images for religious beliefs is to continue the work of painters and poets, musicians and dramatists, who down the centuries have attempted to clothe the ineffable in forms by which it can be understood and passed on.

From the work of the early middle ages to that of Stanley Spencer, it has seemed natural for the scenes of the gospels to be portrayed in the dress and surroundings of the painter's own time. The lazy option, however, is always to fall back nostalgically on the images of past generations, particularly when they are thought of as belonging to the golden age of faith. So in religious television programmes, the graphics artists will tend all too often to turn first to their ecclesiastical Gothic typefaces, the studio designers to their stained glass colours, and the picture researchers to Michelangelo. But that, I believe, is to miss the real opportunity to express the Christian faith powerfully to our own generation. In one BBC1 series of worship programmes designed expressly for television, I made it a discipline that no traditional religious imagery should be used at all, so that the viewers could be invited to worship in the context of their own century and be freed from automatic association of Christianity with the past. And to emphasize the point, the series was called *This Is the Day*.

In this process of finding illuminating imagery, we are following in the footsteps of theologians who are concerned in this process by which concepts are incarnated in images. When we speak about God, heaven or salvation, how can we speak in anything but metaphors and similes? 'God is our heavenly father.' 'Paradise is like a garden.' 'We have been redeemed like a slave from bondage.' But metaphors can only function if the terms they employ are true to the experience of those who use them. Redemption is now a dead metaphor, suggesting a sad transaction in a pawnbroker's rather than a joyful liberation. Even the fatherhood of God must now find a form that can include the motherhood of God. This is the task of any theology that is truly creative: the minting of new metaphors of the transcendent, of new forms for the archetypes. And there is no reason why this work should not be undertaken with the medium of film and television as much as with any other.

I made an attempt to do this in the 1984 BBC2 series, *The Sea of Faith*. Here are a couple of examples of how this process of putting ideas into pictures worked.

In the programme on the thought of Carl Jung, I struggled for a long time to find appropriate imagery for the passage on his attitude to the idea of God:

> The idea of an all-powerful, divine Being is present everywhere, unconsciously, if not consciously, because it is an archetype. I therefore consider it wiser to acknowledge the idea of God consciously; for, if we do not, something else is made God, usually something quite inappropriate and stupid such as only an 'enlightened' intellect could hatch forth.[7]

Beyond being quite certain that any kind of cinematic special effects were out of the question, I did not know at all how to approach this passage about the divine Being present everywhere. Hollywood has accustomed us to the notion that the presence of God can only be conveyed by a CGI Shekinah effect of heavenly light, together with a sepulchral voice to which a lot of echo has been added, presumably because God is speaking from a long way away in the vault of heaven. But this surely leaves a modern audience with a strong impression that the experience of God is as implausible as science fiction, since it requires exactly the same kind of film trickery before it can be imagined.

By contrast, I was looking for an image that came from the real world but heightened our perception of it. Nothing came to me, even after we had begun filming at Jung's lakeside house at Bollingen – until I noticed that the trees above his meditation tower were being washed with sunlight reflected up from the lake. Jung himself must have watched the way the waves of light suffused the whole scene with 'a sense sublime of something far more deeply interfused' that 'rolls through all things' (to use Wordsworth's words). It seemed the perfect symbol, and we only had to point the camera at it. This image was followed by its opposite, the shadow of the trees, to carry on the contrast in the thought and pick up the tongue-in-cheek use of the term 'enlightened' intellect.

When it came to the sixth and final programme in *The Sea of Faith* series, the philosopher Ludwig Wittgenstein provided an even greater challenge. How to achieve a heightening of perception while using imagery from the world that was so important to him: everyday life in the city of Cambridge? I decided on an extreme solution and set fragments of his spiritual reflections in the context of Woolworths, a store of which he was said to be fond, and which offered interesting possibilities. So, we put together images normally thought banal – scrubbing brushes and balls of string – with words like these: 'God grant the philosopher insight into what lies in front of everyone's eyes.'[8] And: 'Not *how* the world is mystical, but *that* it is.'[9]

And then we filmed a toy clown on a trapeze together with Nigel Osborne's haunting score for Wittgenstein's conclusion: 'This can come about only if you no longer rest your weight on the earth, but suspend yourself from heaven. Then everything will be different.'

The resulting sequence was derided by some critics, but for me it was more true to the spirit of Wittgenstein's experience than the traditional imagery they were expecting. And was it more than an urban equivalent of Blake's way of seeing 'a world in a grain of sand, and a Heaven in a wild flower?'[10] But the critics' reaction was equally legitimate. Although the roots of imagery may go deep into the collective unconscious, all responses to it are subjective. All I felt I could do was to provide a sufficient richness of imagery for viewers to be at least offered a ride beneath the surface of things; what connections they made were up to them.

I don't want to claim too much for the particular series *The Sea of Faith*, but I do want to make high claims for the potential of film and television in the creation of contemporary religious images, metaphors and myths. Christianity in particular is in desperate need of just this form of refreshment of its central tenets. This process may operate at its highest level in the work of religious prophets and the poets of the inner life, but I see no reason why it should not extend to popular culture as well.

Here is a handful of examples from my own experience. The 1965 John Robinson book *Honest to God* brought home to me, as it must have done to millions of others, that God could no longer be thought of as a bearded old man in the sky. To discard the old image was a liberation – but what was to replace it? Robinson suggested 'the Ground of Being'. I do not think we were impressed. We were asking for bread and had been given a philosophical stone. It is not enough to point out that an outworn metaphor is only a metaphor, nor is it sufficient to replace it with an abstract formulation. If all language about God is metaphorical, then we need new metaphors.

With little on offer from the official guardians of the faith, it was left to an unlikely prophet from California, the director George Lucas, to come up with something that actually spoke to ordinary people. The film *Star Wars* involved a developed theology with a very vivid metaphor for God, as the unseen Force towards good in the universe. Christian friends of mine happily adopted the greeting 'May the Force be with you'. And the metaphor was worked out in some detail within the film, so that hundreds of millions of viewers were confronted with the idea that 'letting go to the power of the Force within you' might be a better way to defeat evil than to try too hard in one's own strength. I do not remember anyone in the cinema laughing or booing at this essentially Pauline concept.

To put the matter at its simplest, Christian insights are most powerful when they are clothed in the particular metaphorical language appropriate to the contemporary culture. The task is not to de-mythologise, but to re-mythologise.

This may seem hopelessly haphazard to theologians who try to systematise religious language. But if, as I argue, metaphors are always changing, then it makes no sense to ask: 'Is Christ really the Lamb of God, or the Son of God?' Even worse is to embody such systems in creeds and make them a criterion for orthodoxy: 'Is Christ of one substance with the Father, or of like substance?'

For although I part company with Don Cupitt in that I believe that religious myths and metaphors must, if they are to be of any value, refer to an objective rather than to a subjective reality, there is no possible process by which they can be checked against it. The claim of a particular metaphor to be helpful, rather than unhelpful, is subjective, and can only rest on its coherence within a total pattern that makes sense of the universe to each individual.

If, then, we are to be free of the constraints of past creedal formulations, is there to be any check on the riotous imagination of the film-maker or the creative theologian? Yes, and it is an automatic process. The poems we write, the music we compose, the videos we make are all transmitted into the digital ether, usually with no official imprimatur, to be accepted or rejected by whoever happens to come across them. If they touch some chord in the viewer or listener, if some fresh image brings alive what was previously dead, then the artist has spoken from the collective unconscious to the collective unconscious, and may have made some small contribution to the contemporary expression of Christian faith. If this does not happen, it was just another try.

Which Brings Us to Jesus

Who do men say that I am?
Mark 8.27

'Do you speak English?'

'Yes.' The boy who's stopped me looks about 16.

'Can I ask you a question?'

'Sure.'

'What does Jesus mean to you?'

Now there's a shock. Not what I was expecting. Though not such a surprise perhaps given that we are in Taizé, the very unusual monastery in rural France that I've been coming to off and on for 50 years, always trying to get closer to what I believe. And today my questioner is one of around 5,000 young people here for Easter.

'The most inspiring man that ever lived,' I reply.

A safe answer, avoiding any slick piety. But disappointing because he had asked exactly the question I need to answer here. If I'd taken more time to give a considered answer, I might have said: 'The most inspiring man who ever lived, who showed us the way to become sons of God, so that, like him, we can transcend even death and enter into eternal life here and now.' But if that is what I think I believe – and after 65 years of reflection and experience – does it make sense?

In the '70s I made a couple of long investigative programmes – one for radio, one for BBC TV – called 'Who was Jesus?'[1] They established the basics. There is plenty of evidence from contemporary sources separate from the Bible that a man called Jesus of Nazareth worked as a teacher and healer in first-century Palestine and was crucified under Pontius Pilate. There were many people like him at the time. But the content of his teaching seems to have been very special: a programme for authentic moral and spiritual living that is widely respected by the most sceptical of Christians and by many secular humanists. And critical analysis of the gospel texts helps authenticate the key aspects of that teaching.

But then a layer of interpretation was added to his life by the early church that makes extraordinary supernatural claims for him. He was born of a virgin. He performed miracles. He claimed to be both the Messiah and the Son of God. After his death he was resurrected. To which claims my own conclusions would be: No, No, No, and – perhaps surprisingly – Yes.

So, first, what about the virgin birth? Learning from my theological training at Oxford and from the scholars we interviewed for the BBC programmes, it's clear that the whole nativity story was invented out of material from the Old Testament, all designed to show that Jesus was the expected Messiah. And the origin of the virgin birth notion seems to have come from a mistranslation of one of the Old Testament prophesies. The word *almah,* translated as *virgin* in the famous prophecy, 'Behold a virgin shall conceive and bear a son,' simply means *a young woman*. Hebrew has a word for virgin, *bethulah,* but this is not used. I could go on and on about this, but anyway there's no advantage to Jesus being born of a virgin, unless you make weird connections between sex and sin.

In fact, the whole nativity story looks very clearly invented out of Old Testament fragments written hundreds of years before Jesus was born. Here's how this process is summarized in the book *Who Was Jesus?*[2] that I wrote with Don Cupitt. We start with the unlikely setting for Jesus' birth: Bethlehem rather than Nazareth. His birth is only set there because of the book of Micah:

> Thou **Bethlehem**... out of thee shall he come forth unto me that is to be ruler in Israel. (Micah 5:2)

And so with the other elements of the familiar Christmas story, all with Old Testament antecedents:

> There shall come a **star** out of Jacob, and a scepter shall rise out of Israel. (Numbers 24:17)
>
> Behold a **virgin** shall conceive, and bear a son and shall call his name Immanuel. (Isaiah 7:14)
>
> The **ox** knoweth his owner, and the **ass** his master's **crib**.' (Isaiah 1:3)
>
> And the **Gentiles shall come** to thy light, and **kings** to the brightness of thy rising. (Isaiah 60:3)
>
> The kings of Tarshish and of the isles shall **bring presents**: the kings of Sheba and Seba shall **offer gifts**.(Psalm 72:10)

Of course, it's not that the gospel writers Matthew and Luke were trying to fool us into believing fake history. These are theological not historical accounts. As one of my former BBC radio colleagues Peter de Rosa points out in his book *Jesus who became Christ*,[3] they are writing decades after Jesus' death, when he was believed by the early Christian Church to have demonstrated by his resurrection that he was the Son of God. So they are describing how a Son of God *must have been born* – the only way it could have happened given who he turned out to be. And to do so they wove together stories out of the only fabric they knew – the beliefs of their age and imagery of the Old Testament. That's fine and it may have spoken powerfully to the readers of the time. The problem for us it that these are not the ways we would now expect divinity to express itself in a person. Being born of a virgin or walking on water are just not how we expect to recognize his divine nature to show itself. Here again we need newly-minted language, if we are to express for our age what the gospel writers expressed for theirs.

So if the nativity story is not historical, what about the miracles that Jesus is supposed to have performed? Many of the most spectacular are, again, constructed from the Old Testament. To take one example: the story of the feeding of the five thousand that occurs in the gospels. Jesus is preaching to a hungry crowd and suggests that his disciples distribute food to them. They say this is impossible as they have only a few fish and loaves of bread (in John's gospel, this is described as barley bread). But Jesus insists, everyone is miraculously fed, and food is even left over.

More than five hundred years before the gospels were written or Jesus had lived, the editor of the Book of Kings set down this story about the prophet Elisha:

> A man came bringing twenty loaves of barley, and fresh ears of grain in his sack, and Elisha said, 'Give to the men that they may eat.' But his servant said, 'How am I to set this before a hundred men?' So he repeated, 'Give them to the men that they may eat, for thus saith the 'Lord.' 'They shall eat and have some left.' So he set it before them. And they ate, and had some left, according to the word of the Lord.[4]

So either the gospel story was lifted from the Book of Kings, or Jesus decided to restage it. Hm...

Miracles in the Bible – and indeed in some modern thinking – are taken as signs that the person performing them has God on their side. Moses changes a staff into a snake and the Egyptians are amazed. All very pre-scientific, all very conjuring-trick. In fact, Jesus is reported as castigating his generation for always wanting a sign. Rather, when he is asked directly about his credentials as a teacher and prophet, he replies not with a list of miracles, but with a mission statement of social action: 'To preach the good news to the poor… to free those who are oppressed.'[5] No need, at least for me, to believe in implausible miracles like walking on water. Indeed, I would be far less drawn to Jesus if he had been showing off as a miracle worker.

The central question about the historical Jesus is: Did he believe he was the Son of God? According to the gospel writers, he seems to have referred to himself as both 'son of man' and 'son of God'. This leads us straight into the central claim of traditional Christianity: that Jesus was a divine being, the only-begotten Son of God, begotten before all worlds. This in turn almost forces us to take the first step into the doctrine of the Trinity, God in three persons. And it is quickly further elaborated into the full-blooded doctrine of God's master plan.

This doctrine, constructed from Old Testament, Greek, Egyptian and scores of other metaphysical traditions, is a wonderfully fanciful story. God created the world but the first humans He made, Adam and Eve, sinned and passed on that primal curse of sin to all of us. God chose a people, Israel, but they sinned too. He sent prophets to enlighten people, but they were ignored. Finally, he sent His Son whom He had begotten before the beginning of time, to become a human in the womb of a virgin through the action of another person of the Godhead, the Holy Spirit. This Jesus was fully God and fully man. He performed miracles that defied the laws of nature, such as walking on water and rising from the dead after he was killed. He then ascended physically up into the sky to rejoin the other two members of the Holy Trinity. And Jesus will come back to earth one day to judge the living and the dead. It was essential to the plan that Jesus die, because his death was a blood sacrifice through which God forgave us our sins by punishing him in our place with the death we deserved. If you believe all this, you will go to heaven and if you don't you will go to hell.

That is the simple story that centuries of our Christian ancestors managed to believe and that a few still affirm today, at least on Sundays during the recital of the creed. But is it any wonder that most people take one look at it and say, 'If that's your good news, you can keep it! And by the way, please don't teach it to my children.' To me too this is a horrible story – as horrible as the story of God asking Abraham to sacrifice his own son as a loyalty test. Very Mafia.

How did this come about? How did the church re-invent the man Jesus of Nazareth as Jesus Christ, the divine second person of the Trinity? Don Cupitt puts it well:

> What the Church did was personify the teaching in the cult of the Teacher, seeing Jesus as embodying his own message. He preached the Kingdom; the Church said he is the King. He preached God's salvation: the Church said he is the Saviour. He preached the grace of God and called for faith in God: the Church said he is the gracious gift of God to men, and called for faith in him... It has always been much easier to worship the Godman enthroned in heaven than to face up to the real message of Jesus himself.[6]

But to say that Jesus was fully human is not to say a little about him but to say a lot. It is to say that he expressed the full flowering of our humanity: how a human being created in the image of God can recapture that divine spark in themselves and live it out to its full, extraordinary potential. So what makes much more sense to me is to think of Jesus not as *the* Son of God, but as *a* son of God. After all, in the Bible, other people – like King David – are called sons of God. Psalm 82 proclaims: 'All of you are children of the Most High.' And Jesus' own prayer that he is said to have taught us to use starts '*Our* Father'. Doesn't that imply that we are all sons of God? Jesus is for me quite simply the most perfect example of just what a son of God can be.

In talking like this, I am opening myself to centuries of heretical thinking of the kind that convulsed the early Church.

My particular heresy was called 'adoptionism' – the idea that Jesus was a man of such spiritual calibre that he was recognized as a son of God, a son by adoption. And that this opportunity is there for all of us.

In fact, on the subject of Jesus I probably qualify for all the main kinds of heresy in church history, and therefore must be a clear candidate for burning at the stake. Here's the charge against me.

I'm an *adoptionist* – the man Jesus was adopted as son of God – like many others and even like us.

I am an *Ebionite* – Jesus was a prophet with his divine nature expressed at his baptism.

I am *gnostic* – not saved through Jesus' death but through the understanding he brought through his life. And we can follow him, each of us with our own spark of the divine. Once again, the real God is not the Old Testament God but 'the unknown God'.

There's an excellent summary of all these heretical interpretations of the nature of Jesus in Frédéric Lenoir's book *Comment Jésus est devenue Dieu*[7] (How Jesus became God). It comes as some comfort to us heretics that the etymology of heretic is 'one who is able to choose'.

You might think from the constant repetition of 'Father, Son and Holy Spirit' in almost every church service, that I would be seen as an unusual sort of heretic by most Christians. But, perhaps surprisingly, a Gallop poll in 2003[8] showed that among baptized Christians in Europe only between 20 per cent and 40 per cent actually believed in the doctrine of the Trinity.

But I am about to shock the humanists who thought I was on their side in my view of Jesus as a man like us. This is because I am also saying that the aim of the religious life is to become divine ourselves in the same way that Jesus was divine. Before you remind me about pharaohs and Roman emperors who thought they were gods, let me surprise you further by saying that this idea of 'divinization', or '*theosis*', is actually what the

Eastern Orthodox church has always taught. St Athanasius put it very simply: 'God became man so that men might become gods.'[9] The Orthodox Archdiocese of North America puts it rather sweetly like this:

> Does this not get you just a little bit excited? Does it not describe something more than 'being saved' or 'going to heaven when I die'? Is your heart racing just a little? If so, you are starting to grasp *theosis* (becoming divine). It is an understanding of our purpose as believers that is not just Orthodox, it is thoroughly biblical.[10]

Or as Karen Armstrong puts it in describing this Orthodox view: 'The man Jesus gave us our only hint of what God was like and had shown that human beings could participate in some indefinable way in the being of the incomprehensible God.'[11]

This idea of divinization was not only believed but also described shockingly bluntly by someone usually thought of as a mainstream Western Christian, C.S. Lewis:

> It is a serious thing to live in a society of possible gods and goddesses, to remember that the dullest and most uninteresting person you talk to may one day be a creature which, if you saw it now, you would be strongly tempted to worship.[12]

The same thought is there in the *Namaste* greeting, popularly translated as 'the divinity in me honours the divinity in you'.

So, am I a Christian or not in what I believe about Jesus? I certainly don't believe that Jesus was 'the only begotten Son of God, begotten of His Father before all worlds'. It's only by abandoning such beliefs that I can find Christianity credible at all. Rather, I am a Christian in the sense of being a follower of the man Jesus – in the same way as a Marxist is a follower of Marx, not someone who worships Marx as God. Nevertheless, for my own brand of Christian agnosticism, Jesus is central. That's what makes it Christian agnostic rather than Buddhist agnostic, etc., and central to the Jesus whom I follow is the teaching that he lived out with total integrity.

So what was the essence of Jesus' teaching? For me it has two dimensions: teaching about ethics and teaching about the meaning of life. It's vital to include both. Otherwise it's all too easy to reduce the good news of Christianity to the familiar trope that we're happy to acknowledge the value of Christian ethics with its love-thy-neighbour ideals, but let's please leave out all the God-talk.

The gospels are, as we've seen, a mixture of things Jesus may have said and things that the early Church thought he should have said. But you can't miss the main thrust of the highly original stories Jesus told: the parables like the Prodigal Son or the Good Samaritan that make unforgettable the values of selfless generosity, justice for the marginalized, and the poison of judgemental attitudes.

Perhaps the essence of Jesus' teaching is best seen from its opposite. I can't think of a better summary than this brilliant meme on Facebook, with its ironic teaching of 'Alt-Jesus':

Fear everyone
Expel the stranger
Blame the poor
Ignore the sick
Feed the rich
Love only thyself
Trust only Caesar
Throw lots of stones.

But, important as ethics are, for me being a Christian is far more than being a follower of Jesus' teaching. You can follow rules in an external way, in an unloving way, and without any fundamental change in who you are. Jesus was about that fundamental change. A change so total it can hardly be overstated: being born again, dying as a caterpillar and being reborn as a butterfly, living eternal life now, letting the divine spark catch fire, becoming Christ-like, becoming a son of God.

The story of the transfiguration of Jesus on the mountain top is a symbolic image of what happens when we encounter the divine and are transfigured by it, when our spiritual body begins to shine through. The collect for the Sunday when the Transfiguration story is read contains this prayer, asking for the same to happen to us as happened to Jesus: 'That we may… be changed into his likeness, from glory to glory.' And the ritual reminder of how we can be touched by the divine comes when we share his body and blood in bread and wine. A very weird idea when considered literally, transfiguring when it begins to work.

But here's another surprising and shocking thing. If this is the essence of Jesus – why he lived, what he struggled and died for, why he is our inspiration – why is none of that in the creed? This is all it typically says about his life:

> I believe in Jesus Christ, his only Son, our Lord,
> who was conceived by the Holy Spirit,
> born of the Virgin Mary,
> suffered under Pontius Pilate,
> was crucified, died, and was buried.

That's it. We affirm simply that he was born and died with an empty gap in between – nothing about his teaching or the way he lived it out. This makes Jesus a cypher, like the classical gods. What is important for the traditional creeds is that the cypher was born by a virgin, died, rose from the dead and ascended into heaven. Those are the necessary steps in the metaphysical storyline: the ingredients necessary to make the dish of salvation. But this is to leave out entirely the main point of Christianity, its Unique Selling Proposition (USP), its good news, its invitation to be reborn. It is extraordinary how the Churches continue to betray the message of Jesus in this way instead of passing it on, struggling to understand its implications and live them out.

I have searched in vain for an official version of the creed that puts the good news that Jesus taught at its heart. But here is a fragment that points the way. It's from James Burklo's *Credo for Christians.*[13]

> I follow the way of Jesus,
> who found God in himself
> and shared a way for others to find God in themselves.
> He was born through love,
> He lived for love,
> He suffered for love,
> He died for love,
> But love never dies.
> I submit myself to the leading of the love that is God,
> that I may be compassionate toward all beings.

So for anyone interested in an invitation to find a path to religious belief with a Christian flavour that is not intellectually compromising, my suggestion would be: bypass the creeds, doctrines and supernaturalism, and start by simply reading about the very surprising life and teaching of Jesus of Nazareth. And don't start with the gospels, where the picture of the man himself has been overlaid with the Church's silver and gold ornamentation. Start rather with fresh re-tellings of the simple story. Among my personal favourites are *The Goodman Jesus and the Scoundrel Christ*[14] by Philip Pullman, *John Mark*[15] by Christopher Epting, and *It Happened in Palestine*[16] by Leslie Weatherhead.

A final thought from Don Cupitt on the importance of the message of Jesus:

> His message is beginning to be better understood, though there is a long way to go yet, and there is no sign that the Churches are willing to face up to the implications. All previous reforms or renewals of Christianity, by men like Augustine and Luther, Wesley and Karl Barth, have been rediscoveries of Paul's developed theology. Perhaps next time Jesus himself will reform Christianity. He is long overdue.[17]

The Spark

> *The worst danger for Christianity is not heresies, heterodoxies... not free thinking. No, it is the kind of orthodoxy which is hearty twaddle, mediocrity with a dash of sugar.*[1]
> Søren Kierkegaard

What of the Church? Is there any longer any point to it? If the Church is to remain relevant in people's lives, it must have a message and a mission that resonates with us today. Typically, it describes its mission as evangelization, to spread the gospel, the good news. So, what is that 'good news'?

If you ask Wikipedia what this good news is, it contrasts these two very different options:

> In Christianity, the gospel or the Good News, is the news of the coming of the Kingdom of God (Mark 1:14–15). [Alternatively] Paul's gospel is of Jesus' death on the cross and resurrection to restore people's relationship with God.[2]

The second of these, St Paul's version, is the one most often preached in churches today. God has sent his only Son to die on the cross as a blood sacrifice as the only way to atone for the original sin of the whole world. Jesus died on the cross to save me from my sin.

And don't imagine that this form of the good news belongs only to the evangelical wing of the Church. It is right at the heart of the liturgy of Catholics, Orthodox and Protestants. The *Kyrie Eleison* that has been recited and sung for close on two thousand years is addressed to Jesus, the Passover sacrificial lamb slain for us: 'Lamb of God, that takest away the sins of the world, have mercy upon us.' And some of us had the same idea drummed into us in Sunday School with the most popular children's hymns like *There Is a Green Hill,* inviting us to sing about Jesus: 'There was no other good enough to pay the price of sin.' And there are plenty of verses in the New Testament, particularly in the epistles of Paul, expounding this interpretation of the Christian good news.

But if that is the Church's USP, its strapline and mission statement, does it sound like good news to us today? It certainly doesn't to me. For it even to begin to be relevant I would have to feel so irredeemably wicked and sinful that no human remedy would be possible. I would have to believe that I needed a blood sacrifice by God himself to wash away my sins. Finally, I would have to believe that the historical figure of Jesus of Nazareth was that Son of God sent to play out this final plan, since God's earlier plans for humanity had failed. Hmm…

Then there is another version of the good news in the New Testament. The Acts of the Apostles recounts the first days of the embryonic Christian Church, and it characterizes the message that was preached, the kerugma, in only three words: 'Jesus is Lord.' Many theologians believe that this was the original good news that the first Christians proclaimed – and very successfully. But again, this doesn't come across to me personally as good news. I wasn't looking for a Lord. Quite the contrary. If I regress to being a subject, then the moral autonomy I have been taught as so important would have to be surrendered.

Moreover, this develops into a whole way of thinking about the will of God. 'Thy will be done,' we pray, 'on earth as it is in heaven'. Or we concede to God: 'Not as I will, but as Thou wilt.' Or even: 'Your child's death was God's will.' It's a way of thinking built deep into Christian traditional language. At it's most stark, it's there in a hymn written by Timothy Dudley-Smith, based on words of St Augustine. In one line we are invited to pray for 'His will to master mine.'[3] That can't be right, can it? It sounds like the ultimate patriarchy. I hope that's not what the early Christians had in mind when they came up with the strapline *Jesus Is Lord*.

But if we go even further back, there is another characterization of what gospel or good news means. It comes in words put into the mouth of Jesus himself, when he describes his own mission statement: 'The Spirit of the Lord is upon me, because he hath anointed me to preach the gospel to the poor.'[4] Such preaching of the good news was not merely to be expressed in words but in actions: 'He hath sent me to heal the brokenhearted, to preach deliverance to the captives, and recovery of sight to the blind, to set at liberty them that are bruised.' I'm going to slide over for the moment the awkward fact that Jesus typically called this new reality the *Kingdom* of God. 'Kingdoms' carry negative connotations for most of us these days, and I'll come back to this in the next chapter. Let's for now call it a new 'era' that is arriving.

So, the good news that Jesus is telling us is that a new era is arriving – God is inviting us to be part of it, here and now. We don't have to wait until we are perfect, or until we are dead. We can enter into a fullness of life, of joy through self-giving, of love that is stronger than death. Which sounds to me like the best possible news. That my life, far from being 'solitary, poor, nasty, brutish, and short'[5] (as Hobbes characterized it), or absurd and meaningless (as Sartre would have it), has the potential to be glorious.

And Jesus himself is the centre of this good news, because he not only proclaimed it but lived it. He showed us the way. We see in him how the divine spark can catch fire into a life of blazing joy. He proved that it works. And the same divine spark already in all of us can catch fire from him, like the candle flame passed from person to person until the whole church is full of light. We can join in the prayer to our common Father, growing into the divine nature that we can share with Jesus as children of God, sons and daughters of God like Jesus himself. Now that *is* good news.

A good theory, you may say, but where can I see it working for real? Where is the proof of this divine pudding? That's a question to struggle with. I can find communities where it is discussed intellectually. The Sea of Faith Network, which developed from the original *Sea of Faith* television programmes, is one example. The Progressive Christian Alliance is another. And I have seen it in many radiant individual Christians, saints even, like Dom Hélder Câmara, the late Bishop of Recife in Brazil, who chose to live in solidarity with the poorest. He famously wrote: 'If I give bread to the poor, they call me a saint. If I ask why they are poor, they call me a communist.'[6] His example led me to resign my job as Head of Religious Television at the BBC to focus on making films that might answer Dom Hélder Câmara's question: 'Why are they poor?'

But I have struggled to find a community to join that combines progressive theology with forms of liturgy that take me deeper and deeper to experience personally the heart of the Christian good news – an invitation to realize our divine destiny, our vocation to take on something of the glory of Jesus. There is one such place that so inspired me that I spent most of one year living there, wondering whether to give up everything and join the community. But let me go back to the beginning of my muddled journey through the byways of the Christian Church. It is clearly presumptuous for anyone to pass judgement on two millennia of the Christian Church, so the only way I can approach it is to share some reflections on how my journey in and out of different churches has evolved over seventy years.

I was dedicated (rather than baptized) under the flag of the Salvation Army in working class Wandsworth. My grandparents on both sides were staunch Salvationists, as were my mother and my aunt. Up to the age of six, I loved the warm and enthusiastic atmosphere of the meetings, with the brass band playing and choruses that were fun to sing: 'Jesus bids us shine with a clear, pure light, like a little candle burning in the night.' Everything

I learned about Christianity in those days was through those choruses. They contained moral lessons that were simple to understand. 'Jesus first, myself last and others in between.' But above all they contained stories of Jesus: simple stories that he told and the stories of what he did. 'Tell me the stories of Jesus I love to hear, things I would ask him to tell me if he were here.' And nothing wrong with any of that. If there's one good thing to teach young children in terms of religion, it would be the stories of Jesus: from the Good Samaritan to 'let him that is without sin cast the first stone.'[7]

So, on balance I think it was a good start. But I couldn't have stayed in the Salvation Army. If I'd been promoted from Junior Soldier to become a Salvationist, the words of the songs would have changed from 'Jesus wants me for a sunbeam' to 'There is a fountain filled with blood, drawn from Immanuel's veins.' That's the full fundamentalist story that starts with conviction of sin and ends with a blood sacrifice on the cross. The Army was very hot on sin in those days: any drinking, smoking, theatre-going, dancing – almost anything that seemed like fun – was out, especially on a Sunday. I remember how shocked I was when, my mother having decided to go blonde, my grandmother at the kitchen table started singing under her breath: 'You fashionable people, with your pomp and pride, powdered and painted and your hair all dyed, like the label on the bottle, you'll be left outside... When Gabriel blows his silver horn.'[8] It was no wonder my mother decided we needed to find a new church.

So, we became non-conformists, members of Sanderstead Congregational Church for my teenage years. This was intellectually liberating. There was room for all sorts of views from all sorts of people. Even my atheist father was welcomed. Over time he became more and more involved, finding his own very idiosyncratic form of faith and becoming a deacon.

No brass bands here. In the non-conformist world, it was all about preaching. I went to hear the great preachers of the day:

Donald Soper and Leslie Weatherhead. It is hard to believe now, but at that time in the 1960s there were queues around the block to get into Leslie Weatherhead's preaching in the huge City Temple. And that was usually only to get into the overflow hall. There was a different kind of fervour in the air then, and one that led to my thinking that I was called to be a Congregational minister. That is another story, but it ended the same way as I ran into another road block. As a student pastor in a church in Walsall, it became clear that I couldn't provide what the congregation was asking from their minister – a wholehearted endorsement of the entire A to Z of Christian doctrine. I couldn't preach with my whole heart if the Bible passages they so loved were to be my texts.

The non-conformist church tradition that I belonged to at that time was what they called a *ministry of the word,* centred on preaching: the head rather than the heart. That was fine as far as it went. My father later adopted for his coat of arms the motto *Fortiter ad Verbum*: holding strongly to the word. But I was missing the heart side – the mystery, the music that takes you out and away, the silence to fall into.

I found that invitation to *feel* the good news as well as to think about it in Taizé. The time I first went was on a scooter through France to this out of the way village in the Christmas snow, where the original group of around twenty young Protestant monks were living a life of simplicity and welcome, based in a tiny village church. It was an inspiration. And it continues to be so to this day, though now with hundreds of brothers (still no sisters) and tens of thousands of young people travelling from all over the world to take part. Each of the simple three services every day is the same: long silences and quiet chanting by everyone of phrases in different languages. Chants like *Dona nobis pacem in diebus nostris* – give peace in our days. There is almost no preaching, and certainly no creed with a set of propositions that we have to affirm. I was baptized in Taizé at the age of 22. I very nearly joined the community, but finally decided (barely) that that path too wasn't for me. Instead I stayed on in Oxford, studied for a doctorate leading to an invitation to a fellowship in Columbia University, New York – and then abandoned both for a six-week contract in BBC radio.

As the six weeks at the BBC turned into 20 years, I was involved with every sort of church worship. I even invented a couple of new ones specifically for broadcasting. Meditations with the remarkable Dominican monk, Simon Tugwell, involved so much silence that engineers feared the transmitters would shut down. They didn't, and – live on television as well as on radio – millions shared the silence with us.

I felt that television had taken the lazy approach of simply televising church services as events, rather than re-inventing them for the different medium, as if BBC drama consisted only of outside broadcasts from theatres. So, I experimented with *This Is the Day*: a service of Holy Communion where the communion in question was the entire community of the people participating live on television. The first service was conducted by the leading Methodist minister Donald Soper in the front room of a housebound woman in West London. As he broke bread and shared the wine with her, he invited viewers to do the same with their own bread and wine at home. It felt like a breakthrough.

As I used to argue, if the churches always claim to be worshipping with the communion of saints in heaven, why not with the equally invisible but equally real community of television viewers? *This Is the Day* continued for many years, but eventually the familiar church services returned, until today these outside broadcasts have almost all been dropped. Died of boredom, I suspect.

So, is the Church any closer today to finding a USP that represents a life-changing invitation to the coming generations? If so, please let me know.

Love Is the Thing

The Kingdom of God is Justice and Peace, and Joy in the Holy Spirit.
Taizé chant

I want to come back to that tricky idea of the Kingdom of God. Clearly it was a central theme of Jesus' teaching, but equally clearly it sounds discordant to our egalitarian ears. And it's the same problem with the good news that the first apostles proclaimed to the world, that *Jesus is Lord*. The language of both messages seems tied to a feudal, monarchical view that doesn't do it for me. And it gets worse when this leads to a form of worship that essentially invites me to bow down and worship a cosmic king on a heavenly throne and just keep singing his praises. Why? What's in that for Him, never mind me?

But what if I start from a different viewpoint: a different understanding of this puzzling word *God*? These are my clues. 'God is love, and those who dwell in love dwell in God, and God in them.'[1] 'Love came down at Christmas.'[2] Or, as we chant over and over again at Taizé: 'Ubi Caritas et Amor, Deus ibi est.' Maybe it is that simple: God = Love, Love = God.

Let's try starting from this traditional parallelism as though it were a kind of codebook. And let's give Love the same capital letter – nothing wrong with a little neo-Platonism. We can see a spectrum beginning here that may start with love for chocolate biscuits but can end with Love as our ultimate life-value. Orthodox Jews will never say aloud the name of God – YHWH – the four consonants to which Christians add vowels to make Jehovah or Yahweh. Instead, orthodox Jews read the name aloud as 'Lord'. So why can't Christians read it aloud as 'Love'?

Now, using our codebook, Jesus is preaching the *Kingdom of Love*. And the apostles' good news is that *Love rules*. That is indeed a shocking and liberating message to a world where it seems most of the time that what rules is violence, money, power, the laws of physics, and a general meaninglessness. Entropy rather than empathy. And now worship becomes the celebration of Love. Nothing groveling about that. No need to set up separate Sunday assemblies to avoid God talk. No need to exclude popular culture, when every pop song seems to proclaim *Love is the thing*.

And we could use the same translation for the creed.

Credo in unum Deum.

becomes:

I believe in one Love, creating heaven and earth.
And in Jesus Christ, a son of Love.

That's a creed I'd be happy to say every Sunday. And in effect, I already do.

So, the *Kingdom of Heaven* becomes the *Kingdom of Love*. No wonder Jesus says that this kingdom is here and now. Its heaven is here around us in every act of love, right down to the taste of the chocolate biscuit. The flowers of the field, that are here today and gone tomorrow, they too are expressions of God's love, Jesus says. It is all created in love. That's what God's creation of the world means. And it's what gives it its ultimate meaningfulness.

But lest this sound like I'm reducing the Christian message to a no more than celebration of human love, let me repeat that I am saying that love is our best *picture* of God. I am not saying that God is no more than our human *idea* of love. No idea can itself provide the ultimate reassurance and meaningfulness that I need to underpin my life. That requires a power greater than myself or any human agency. It requires God, the ultimate power and meaning of the universe. And what better picture for this God than Love.

It seems to me that this also helps with the two trickiest conundrums in Christian theology.

First, does God act in this world or not? If not, as someone or other put it, 'What is He doing all day?' What is religion for, if it makes no difference to anything in the real world? That does sound like an intractable problem. But I don't feel the same impossibility in saying that Love is in action in the world. She is in action through the every act of human love (the smiles that Pierre Teilhard de Chardin insists are 'never lost'). And Love also moves, we are told, in more mysterious ways – deep in the very fabric of the world we live in. If this is true, then we can say that we do experience the divine in this world; in experiences that many people would understand as akin to religious.

The Anglican divine George Herbert put it perfectly in a poem where 'the Lord' is most definitely 'Love' with a capital L:

Love bade me welcome; yet my soul drew back,
Guilty of dust and sin.
But quick-eyed Love, observing me grow slack
From my first entrance in,
Drew nearer to me, sweetly questioning
If I lack'd anything.

'A guest,' I answer'd, 'worthy to be here':
Love said, 'You shall be he.'
'I, the unkind, ungrateful? Ah, my dear,
I cannot look on Thee.'
Love took my hand and smiling did reply,
'Who made the eyes but I?'

'Truth, Lord; but I have marr'd them: let my shame
Go where it doth deserve.'
'And know you not,' says Love, 'Who bore the blame?'
'My dear, then I will serve.'
'You must sit down,' says Love, 'and taste my meat.'
So I did sit and eat.[3]

What an invitation to the Eucharist, to Holy Communion! And not only in church. In just the same way, as Bishop John Robinson used to say, making love is a form of Holy Communion. We *do* have glimpses of God, without waiting for a voice or a vision: Love *is* at work in the world.

Which brings us to the other great stumbling block that keeps so many people away from any religious belief: how can there be an all-powerful God who doesn't prevent the evils of the world? The question is just as hard when we change the name from God to Love, but it becomes directly meaningful for all of us. How can we believe in the power of Love in the face of an Auschwitz or today's Yemen? That is not a question inviting the answer 'We can't believe', but rather, 'We have to believe'. 'Why isn't God doing anything about it?' becomes 'Why isn't our Love doing enough about it?' For peace-makers like Tolstoy or Mahatma Gandhi, this Love is a paradoxical form of spiritual power that can work in spite of appearances. Jesus' last words on the cross were not 'I'm a blood sacrifice for the sins of future evangelicals,' but words of love for his enemies: 'Father, forgive them, for they know not what they do.'[4]

If we can use this code for many of the traditional formulations of the Church, how about for benediction? When I was asked to give the blessing at two of our grandchildren's naming days, I attempted a translation of the oldest known form of blessing which we have from some 4,000 years ago,[5] so that non-Christians (or progressive Christians) could feel included. Now with this simple codebook, I can put it like this:

> May Love bless you and keep you. May She make Her face to shine upon you and be gracious unto you. May Love lift up the light of Her countenance upon you and give you peace.

It helps with the gender issue as well.

Harder perhaps is the most traditional form of Christian

benediction: 'The blessing of Almighty God, Father, Son and Holy Ghost.' If we feel the Trinitarian form helps, we could try something like this:

> May the blessing of everlasting Love, from the whole creation, through our shared humanity, to your own spirit, be yours this day and for evermore, world without end. Amen.

It would probably sound better in Latin.

If It Means Anything, It Means Everything

Stepping onto a travelator from eternity.[1]
Imogen Cooper on Schubert's last sonata

So, where does this leave us on this ordinary wet Monday morning?

I hope I've explained that as a Christian agnostic I don't *know* anything for certain about God. But that does not mean simply getting on with my life with a personal philosophy in the 'just-don't-know' column, in a way that would make religion irrelevant. That would leave me with a sense of meaninglessness that I couldn't live with. I am not just a *so-what* agnostic, I am a *Christian* agnostic. In the religious area, I may not know stuff but I certainly believe stuff. I believe that the universe exists for a purpose, that my life – and everyone's life – counts, that love is integral to life's meaning, and that all this is not thrown away at the point of death.

That's my guess about God. But I can't leave it at that – as an intellectual position only, my version of Pascal's bet. Its whole point is that it underlies the very meaning of my life. I may not have evidence that it is true, but if it is true, then it is the most important reality that confronts us and underpins everything. **If it means anything, then it means everything**.

In the few years when I was training for the ministry of the United Reformed Church, I had to preach sermons in Mansfield College, Oxford, and in tiny free churches of Oxfordshire. And my favourite text to preach on was the challenge that Joshua put to the people of Israel:

> Choose you this day whom you will serve… whether the gods your fathers served in the region beyond the River. But as for me and my house, we will serve the Lord.[2]

It's a choice. Choose you this day whom you will serve. If we have placed our life-chip on the guess of a meaningful universe, and called the ground of that meaning 'God', then we have to follow through.

But how? For Joshua and Moses, it was an idea of serving God. And that in turn can be simplified back to following His commandments. And strangely, I find a version of this idea works for me too. But I need to take a step back.

If it's true that we all have some kind of primitive religious 'gene', some archetypal tendency to religiosity, then certainly its earliest manifestations were anything but attractive. The oldest idea seems to have been that religion was a question of placating the gods that were the controllers of the natural world, in order to persuade them to protect us from storms or ensure fertility. And to achieve that we had to placate them in the same way that we would placate any powerful ruler – with presents like sacrificed animals and a lot of flattery.

This approach to God suffuses not only the Bible but also much of contemporary Church worship. What otherwise is the point of seeing the crucifixion of Jesus as 'the sacrifice once offered for the sins of the world'? What otherwise is the point of endlessly singing to God 'How great Thou art'? If there is God, then I can't see Him being particularly happy about being surrounded by choirs of angels and saints, endlessly singing 'Holy, holy, holy, Lord God Almighty, etc., etc., etc.' It would be like being condemned to watch endless editions of *Songs of Praise*. If this is what your God really wants as the ultimate purpose of His universe, then I can only agree, as I quoted before, with the great cry in Ibsen's play *Brand*: 'Your God is too small!'

Although probably every monk and nun in Christendom will disagree with me, I can't see that the first response to believing in God should be committing ourselves to endlessly worshipping Him – either here on earth or throughout eternity in the courts of heaven.

But there is another, opposite theme in the Old Testament that offers a different approach to how to live in alignment with the meaning we are guessing at. It's perfectly expressed by the prophet Amos:

> Thus saith the Lord, I hate, I despise your feasts, and I take no delight in your solemn assemblies. Even though you offer me your burnt offerings and grain offerings, I will not accept them; take away from me the noise of your songs; to the melody of your harps I will not listen. But let justice roll down like waters, and righteousness like an ever-flowing stream.[3]

Or as another prophet, Micah, put it: 'To do justice, and to love kindness, and to walk humbly with your God.'[4]

This suggests that the follow-through response to believing in God is to act morally. However, we must be careful here. My own sense of Christian morality does not come down to obeying versions of the Ten Commandments or avoiding the deadly or non-deadly sins. Deeper morality is pretty much the opposite of that, as Jesus pointed out. Christian ethics was the subject of my Oxford D.Phil. But that was never completed, even after the two years of residence and research. That is probably just as well, because when it comes to moral philosophy my thinking has moved on. Today, I see the point of Christian ethics not as rules in the head, but as the state of one's heart. For me the key saying of Jesus is: 'Every good tree produces good fruit; but the corrupt tree produces evil fruit.'[5] We must look behind our actions to the kind of person we are that naturally gives rise to those actions. As Eduard Schweizer, a Swiss New Testament scholar, put it: 'A transformed heart produces a transformed life.'[6]

But how can our hearts be transformed? This brings us back to that extraordinary idea that we can be born again as sons of God: born into eternity here and now, reborn by God's grace, our hearts growing more Christ-like, our lives becoming more fruitful. All these steps are brought together in one verse of a hymn by Christopher Wordsworth, nephew of William:

> Christ is risen, we are risen;
> Shed upon us heavenly grace,
> Rain, and dew, and gleams of glory,
> From the brightness of thy face;
> That we, with heads in heaven,
> Here on earth may fruitful be.[7]

So what is our motivation for this approach to living the religious life? We may no longer be trying to placate and propitiate God, but a lot of traditional religious thought links our moral motivation for what we should do to demonstrate gratitude for what God has done for us. This is a major theme in the Bible. In the Old Testament it was the Exodus story:

Thus saith the Lord God of Israel, I brought your fathers out of Egypt:... and the Egyptians pursued after your fathers with chariots and horsemen unto the Red Sea. And when they cried unto the Lord, he... brought the sea upon them, and covered them. And I brought you into the land of the Amorites, which dwelt on the other side of Jordan; and they fought with you: and I gave them into your hand, that ye might possess their land; and I destroyed them from before you... therefore fear the Lord, and serve him in sincerity and in truth.[8]

In one strain of the New Testament our thankfulness is in response to what God had done in sending His Son to die for us. In everyday church worship it is in response to what He continues to do in an immensely down to earth way. We may plant the corn 'but it is fed and watered by God's almighty hand. He sends the snow in winter, the warmth to swell the grain'. That's what He has done for us, so we should give back in response 'that which Thou desirest, our humble, thankful hearts.'[9]

But I don't believe in a God who acts in the world in this

practical way: destroying the Amorites, watering the corn or changing things in response to my latest prayers. If He were a ruler, that would make Him the most arbitrary of rulers – open to special pleading, mass lobbying and even bribery. We wouldn't stand for it in a local government official.

There was a powerful example of this idea of the point of praying when I was back in church in Mezzolombardo in North Italy. The reading from Luke's gospel was the parable supposedly given by Jesus. It was introduced by Luke's explanation that the parable was intended 'to show the necessity of praying without ceasing'. In the story, a widow can't get justice from a judge, but she goes on and on at him until he concludes that he'd better give her what she wants, or she'll never stop bothering him. And the conclusion in the reading is: 'And will not God bring about justice for his chosen ones, who cry out to him day and night? Will he keep putting them off?'[10] From which we are supposed to conclude that if we go on enough at God with our personal requests, He will eventually accede and change the way the world is going in order to avoid being endlessly bothered. Ough!

So I have to reject these tit-for-tat arrangements that promise that if I obey God's supposed rules, He will intervene for my personal benefit. If I keep going to church, God will answer my prayers and keep me and my family safe in a dangerous world.

But what about a different kind of gratitude: thankfulness for the world just as it is, without any special favours? 'For the beauty of the earth, for the beauty of the skies.' Or: 'It's a wonderful world.' This seems to me more solid ground. I am indeed grateful for this wonderful life I have been given. Alan Bennett says the one thing he misses now that he has given up on religion is having someone to thank when ordinary life goes well.

It seems natural to express that gratitude by celebrating our wonderful world in music, in painting (photography in my case), and even, yes, by thanking God for all of it. And out of the gratitude comes a determination to make life wonderful for our fellows on this planet – human, animal or plant. Now, it seems to me, we are moving towards an authentic motivation for moral action. 'Reverence for life' was the formulation that another of my heroes, Dr. Albert Schweitzer, arrived at as the basis for how one should and could live. And he personally lived it out to the full, taking up medicine in order to promote health in equatorial Africa in the most practical and sensitive ways. And still playing Bach on a battered piano – to date the ultimate expression of Christianity in music. Given everything he had sacrificed from his glittering career in Europe, he certainly chose whom to serve.

Another of my musical heroes, the pianist Murray Perahia, believes something similar about Bach. To understand Bach, he says:

> You have to think in terms of God. He's celebrating God, and celebrating life... And there's such a sense of thankfulness... I think that when one plays Bach, no matter what one's religious feelings are, in Bach you become religious. There is no way around it. You can't be an atheist and you have to accept what religion can give to man.[11]

In a similar way, András Schiff describes the effect of his habit of starting every day by playing an hour of Bach whenever he can find a piano. He says: 'To be able to start the day like this cleanses the soul.'[12]

This experience can open to anyone, believer or not. Marghanita Laski enjoyed calling herself a Church of England atheist. Her particular favourite church service, as it is for many people, was Choral Evensong. And central to that service is the *Magnificat*: the legend of Mary's response to the news that she is to give birth to Jesus. Her soul, Mary says, magnifies the Lord because He has done wonderful things. But notice that these are future things. 'He hath put down the mighty from their seat: and hath exalted the humble and meek.' This is certainly not in either the past or the present tense. The mighty are still very much on their seats, and the meek have yet to inherit the earth. Rather it's a mission statement for how it should be, how it will be, how it represents the deep pattern in the meaning of the world: the love that is the ultimate goal towards which everything is tending (if painfully slowly).

The other central prayer of Evensong is the *Nunc Dimittis*: 'Lord now letteth Thy servant depart in peace, for mine eyes have seen...' In other words, we can let go something of our anxiety about the state of the world because the long view that we take at the end of the earthly lives is that love conquers all. 'All shall be well and all manner of thing shall be well,'[13] as Julian of Norwich said. Or as Pierre Teilhard de Chardin put it: 'The most telling and profound way of describing the evolution of the universe would undoubtedly be to trace the evolution of love.'[14]

Suddenly, this week as I am writing these pages, life offers me what I can only describe as a direct religious experience of this kind.

I'm in the Festival Hall for a recital by one of our favourite pianists, Mitsuko Uchida. I've enjoyed the first half without feeling anything out of the ordinary beyond enjoying the wonderful music. But then, after the interval, the audience hushes as she sits down to play Schubert's B-Flat Major Sonata, the last piece he wrote just weeks before his death at the age of 31. And then for the next I know not how long, time stood still.

Here's how I tried to describe my experience in notes scribbled down later that night:

> Audience as one – the roar of gratitude as the final chord fades away. A wave of love goes on and on.
>
> I'm overcome with Gemeinschaftsgefühl.
>
> I feel cleared and clear.
>
> Surprised by joy.

A glimpse of harmony at the centre of everything.

Miksuko receives it all by bowing low, placing her hand on her heart and then opening her arms wide to us all. Sharing everything. Gratitude for everything.

Afterwards I feel completely different. A veil of worry is lifted. It feels like a veil of sorrow that has been there since Boo died has been lifted, gone in this moment.

And not just harmony, but reached through the darkness and dissonance that Schubert wrote and Mitsuko journeyed through with us.

Worries forgotten, transported, taken out of myself. What transport of delight from Thy pure chalice floweth.

Like Pascal – 'everything forgotten except God'.

God in three persons: Schubert the Father, Mitsuko as Jesus the interpreter Son, and the Holy Spirit in the experience of the audience.

Now that I have experienced it, I will be able to look back, remember its fainter echoes.

The feeling was of being 'swept away' and 'cleared'. Taken out of myself by something greater than myself, but still something I could rest on, rely on.

A glimpse of the image of God in Mitsuko. The meaning of transfiguration. The divine shining through.

Beyond a musical experience into private prayer.

Or now that late in life I am playing even a few pages of Schubert's masterpiece, it feels like touching the hem of his garment.

It was not for nothing that we were there.

If you had been there that night, I know you would have felt the same.

Being born again.

Grace.

The way.

The rose garden.

Seeing the light – being in the light.

I don't know what you make of that. I don't know even what I make of it, some weeks later. But whatever it all means, I know how grateful I am to have had such glimpses, such deep encounters, a few rare times like this in my life.

Some weeks after this close encounter with Schubert's B-Flat Major Sonata I stumbled upon a BBC radio programme about the piece in the series *Soul Music*. The opening words by the pianist Imogen Cooper exactly described the sense of revelation I had experienced. 'You are sort of stepping onto a travelator from eternity – and just joining in.'[15]

So here we are coming closer to a different understanding of what could be meant by religious experience. The traditional version contrasts belief in the God of the philosophers as the result of an intellectual argument with the dramatic direct experience of the divine – hearing a voice, perhaps, or seeing a vision or feeling a presence. Rather I am coming to understand religious experience as something experienced through sublime human experiences that we all share. That moment for the enraptured audience at the end of the Schubert's last sonata. T.S. Eliot's moment in the rose garden. The psalmist's song as he surveys the heavens. The act of lovemaking. The touch of the communion wine on the lips. The moments of what Adlerian psychologists call *gemeinschaftsgefühl,* when we feel our deep interconnectedness with all things.

What makes these *religious* experiences is not that they are coming from another reality, but that they point into another dimension of reality and connect us to it. They are glimpses of the divine – the divine in us, the divine all around us, and the divine beyond us. I experience them as full of the ultimate meaning that cannot be lost. They are the deepest experiences of what life is really about. If this is what religious experience is like for the Christian agnostic, then it can help me stop feeling like a second-class citizen because I don't have 'direct' religious experiences, like hearing the voice of God audibly in the way Joan of Arc supposedly did. Religious experience is available to all of us, if our eyes and hearts are open to it.

Two poets in particular express this version of religious experience. William Blake could see:

> Heaven in a Wild Flower,
> Hold Infinity in the palm of your hand
> And Eternity in an hour.[16]

Perhaps because these lines are so familiar, we are blunted to the extraordinary claim Blake is making. Next time I see a wild flower I will really look – it's offering me a glimpse of *heaven*.

This idea is less familiar and even more striking in the poems of Gerard Manley Hopkins, of whom it has been said by the Cambridge academic, Catherine Phillips:

> What he sees around him says something about the nature of God, or the nature of Christ... And therefore sensual interaction with the world is a matter also of his religious faith, of meeting God. Everything he looks at tells him something about Christ.[17]

This is so clear in Hopkins's own lines:

> For Christ plays in ten thousand places,
> Lovely in limbs, and lovely in eyes not his
> To the Father through the features of men's faces.[18]

Meeting God as we meet the world. This is not seeing the Father through the face of Jesus only, but through the faces of all of us, created in God's image.

So I hope my themes have come together: a trusting belief

in the mystery that is God, exultation in the meaningfulness of life, celebration of the wonder of life in art and music, trust that everything we love is not lost in death, commitment to moral and political action, a sense of community in the best of church worship, and the mysterious vocation for each of us to become sons and daughters of God. If that's what it means to be a Christian agnostic, it's certainly not for nothing. It means everything.

Postscript

After struggling to put these thoughts together over a number of years, and feeling rather alone in the process, I've been so heartened to have just now come across a summary of personal belief that resonates strongly with my own. It's the work of a progressive Episcopalian bishop, Christopher Epting. This, he says, is his personal creed.[1]

> I believe in (trust in, not just intellectually assent to) a Power, Force, Rational Principle at the core of the Universe that is the Source of all that is. I believe it has a personal quality (i.e. 'father/mother'). This Power is so much greater than anything we can imagine that, for all practical purposes, it is beyond measure and without limit ('all' powerful… at least in comparison with us).
>
> I believe in (trust in, not just intellectually assent to) a man named Jesus who actually lived and who was 'anointed' by this Power we call God. Uniquely anointed… never been anyone like him, before or since. So especially related is he to that Power/Source that, when we understand him, we understand something of the Power/Source. (Hence, 'only' son – even though we too are sons and daughters of God). I have freely chosen to assent to this Jesus as my 'lord.' Lord of the manor of my life. I am committed to the truth of his teaching and the example of his life.
>
> This Jesus was conceived as an absolutely unique child of God (as are we all) – by God's 'spirit.' His mother was Mary of Nazareth. I have absolutely no idea what her physical state was when he was born, but his birth was special, even unique. I assume Joseph was not the father, but that he

helped raise Jesus.

Jesus proclaimed the absolute reign and sovereignty of God. He was known to be a healer and exorcist and sage. He prayed. He attracted a band of followers but hung around with the wrong people and ultimately challenged both the religious Establishment and the Roman Empire. It got him into trouble with both and also got him arrested, tried, convicted, and executed. This happened in about 29 CE.

Within a few days, his followers experienced him as alive – personally present with them. Some even saw him. The more they reflected on that experience, the more 'God like' he became the closer he seemed to the Power and Force behind it all. They began to believe (and so do I) that, ultimately, his life and teaching is the standard against which we will be measured. His life is the example of what it means to be fully human.

I believe (trust in, not just intellectually assent to) the fact that the Power and Source of it all is alive and active in the universe and world today as something we call 'holy spirit.' It is our connection to the Source. I have chosen to be part of the assembly of Jesus' followers throughout the world. I believe that that community of persons transcends death and that we remain united – through that Power and Source – to all who have died. I believe that their shortcomings, failures, and mistakes, and mine, will not keep us from eternal relationship with the Power/Source of it all because it is all about compassion and self-emptying love.

I believe that, like Jesus, when we die, it is not the end. That there is a continuing (or rather, renewed) existence in the nearer presence of God, and that – like Jesus – we will be 'who we are' in that existence. Not merged into the divine mind in such a way that we lose our unique identities as children of God. And that there is still a connection, somehow, with those we love.

All this (and not much more), I believe.

References

Chapter 1 Well, Are You a Christian or Aren't You?

1. Often attributed to William Blake. More probably a recent concatenation of ideas.
2. Carl Jung in conversation with John Freeman, BBC *Face to Face*, October 1959.
3. Anthony Kenny, *What I Believe*, (London Continuum, 2006) p.47
4. Anthony Kenny, *What I Believe*, (London Continuum, 2006) p.59
5. 1 Corinthians 13.12
6. William Armstrong, Lord Armstrong of Sanderstead, St George's House, Windsor Lecture
7. Carl Jung, *The Red Book*, p. 339

Chapter 2 My Starting Point

1. Paul Tillich, *The Shaking of the Foundations*, (Charles Scribner's Sons, 1948) p.48
2. William Boyd, *The New Confessions*, (Penguin, 2010)
3. Samuel Johnson, *The Works of Samuel Johnson*, 1855 p.332
4. Paul-Henri Thiry, Baron d'Holbach, *The System of Nature or, the Laws of the Moral and Physical World* (*Système de la Nature ou Des Loix du Monde Physique et du Monde Moral*), 1770
5. Albert Camus, *The Myth of Sisyphus*, 1942
6. Prince's Trust eBay Youth Index/You Gov (Online poll of 2,162 adults aged 16–25 between 13 November and 2 December 2018)
7. William Shakespeare *Hamlet* ,1.5 167–8
8. Samuel Wells, *Hanging by a Thread*, Canterbury Press Norwich, 2016, p. 40
9. Francis Spufford, *Unapologetic*, Faber and Faber, 2012, p. 77
10. Iain Dale, Podcast with Giles Fraser, *Confessions*, March 2019

11. Augustine of Hippo, *Confessions,* Lib 1,1–2,2.5,5: CSEL 33, 1–5

Chapter 3 Paths Not Taken

1. Bertrand Russell, *Is There a God?*, 1952
2. Antony Flew, *There Is a God,* HarperOne 2008, pp 88–89
3. Barry Cooper, *Can I really trust the Bible,* The Good Book Company, 2014
4. Romans 3.23
5. Billy Graham Crusade, *The Blood of Jesus,* 1969 https://www.youtube.com/watch?v=bTzoP6L1r6g
6. Francis Spufford, *Unapologetic,* Faber and Faber, 2012, p. 35
7. *The Westminster Confession of Faith*, Chapter 25, para 6
8. Peter Berger, *A Rumour of Angels,* Penguin Books, 1969 p.35
9. Peter Berger, *A Rumour of Angels,* Penguin Books, 1969 p.73

Chapter 4 The Construction of Religious Meaning

1. Karen Armstrong, *The Case for God,* Vintage, 2010, Chapter 1
2. Hebrews 11:1. Attributed to St Paul, although today many scholars think that this is the work of an unknown writer.
3. Ludwig Wittgenstein, *Philosophical Investigations* 246
4. Pierre Teilhard de Chardin, *Le Milieu Divin,* Collins, 1960, p.26

Chapter 5 The Strange Phenomenon of Free Will

1. Georg Christoph Lichtenberg (1742–1799), German physicist, philosopher. *Notebook J*, aph. 249 trans. by R.J. Hollingdale (1990)
2. Shoshana Zuboff , *Talking Politics* podcast, 14 February 2019

Chapter 6 Which Takes Us to Life after Death

1. *The Poems of Arthur Hugh Clough,* Oxford University Press USA, 1986
2. Pierre Teilhard de Chardin, *Le Milieu Divin,* Collins, 1960,

p.26
3. Fyodor Dostoyevsky, *The Brothers Karamazov,* Chapter 11
4. Robert Runcie quoted in Humphrey Carpenter, *Robert Runcie,* Hodder and Stoughton, 1996, p. 57 (quoted from a conversation with John Mortimer)
5. LiveScience October 16 2015
6. *Resurrection,* by the Belgian nun, Soeur Sourire. 'Velasquez and Michelangelo, reunited from afar, /Will be sketching Cro-Magnon man with unmixed joy./To crown their bliss and refresh the hungry,/Cub scouts from Alaska will be selling chocolate ice creams./Blessed Dominic will rediscover St. Francis,/Toasting their friendship in Benedictine.'
7. Pierre Teilhard de Chardin *Le Milieu Divin* Collins, 1960, p.26
8. *The Poems of Arthur Hugh Clough,* Oxford University Press USA, 1986

Chapter 7 The Great All or Nothing

1. Leo Tolstoy, *War and Peace*, Part 3, Chapter 19
2. I John 4:12
3. Virginia Woolf *Letter to her sister Vanessa Bell,* February 1928
4. Exodus 17:13
5. Luke 6:20
6. John 14:2
7. Carl Jung. 2014. *Collected Works of C.G. Jung,* Volume 7: 'Two Essays in Analytical Psychology', Princeton University Press, p. 71
8. Ludwig Wittgenstein, *Tractatus Logico-Philosophicus,* Routledge and Kegan Paul, 1922, 6.44
9. Ludwig Wittgenstein, *Culture and Value,* Oxford, Blackwell, 1960, 63
10. William Blake, *Auguries of Innocence*

Chapter 8 Which Brings Us to Jesus

1. *Who was Jesus?* BBC television programmes,1977, currently available to view here: http://ntweblog.blogspot.com/2017/06/who-was-jesus-1977-is-now-online.html
2. Don Cupitt and Peter Armstrong, *Who was Jesus?* BBC Books, 1977
3. Peter de Rosa, *Jesus who became Christ*, Collins, London 1975
4. 2 Kings 4:43 ff
5. Luke 4:18
6. Don Cupitt and Peter Armstrong, *Who was Jesus?*, BBC Publications, 1977, pp. 86–87
7. Frédéric Lenoir, *Comment Jésus est devenue Dieu*, Librairie Generale Francaise, 2012
8. Gallop Poll, *Worlds Apart, Religion in Canada, Britain, US*, 2003
9. Athanasius Of Alexandria, *De incarnatione*, 54,3, cf. *Contra Arianos*, 1.3910
10. Orthodox Archdiocese of North America, http://ww1.antiochian.org/content/theosis-partaking-divine-nature
11. Karen Armstrong, *The Case for God*, Bodley Head, 2009, p.111
12. C.S. Lewis, *The Weight of Glory*, New York: Macmillan, Collier Books, 1980, p.18
13. James Burklo, *Open Christianity: Home by Another Road*, St Johann Press, 2000
14. Philip Pullman, *The Goodman Jesus and the Scoundrel Christ*, Canongate Canons; Main – Canons edition (21 Sept. 2017)
15. Christopher Epting, *John Mark*, Red Moon Publications, Oklahoma City, 2012
16. Leslie Weatherhead, *It Happened in Palestine*, Hodder & Stoughton, 1937
17. Don Cupitt and Peter Armstrong, *Who was Jesus?*, BBC Publications, 1977, p.88

Chapter 9 The Spark

1. Søren Kierkegaard quoted in The Sea of Faith, Episode 4
2. Wikipedia, https://en.wikipedia.org/wiki/The_gospel
3. Timothy Dudley-Smith, hymn *'Light of the minds that know him'*
4. Luke 4:18
5. Thomas Hobbes, *Leviathan*, p.662
6. Dom Hélder Câmara, cited in Zildo Rocha, *Helder, O Dom: uma vida que marcou os rumos da Igreja no Brasil* (Helder, the Gift: A Life that Marked the Course of the Church in Brazil), P.53
7. John 8:7
8. This is the only reference I can find to the song: https://docsouth.unc.edu/neh/mallory/mallory.xml

Chapter 10 Love Is the Thing

1. I John 4:16
2. Christina Rossetti, *Love Came Down at Christmas,* 1885
3. George Herbert, *Love,* 1593–1632
4. Luke 23:34
5. Numbers 6:24–26

Chapter 11 If It Means Anything, It Means Everything

1. Imogen Cooper, *Soul Music,* BBC Radio 4, 9 January 2019
2. Joshua 24:14–15
3. Amos 5:24
4. Micah 6:8
5. Matthew 7.17
6. Eduard Schweitzer, *The Good News According to Matthew,* John Knox Press, 1975, pp.186–187
7. Christopher Wordsworth, *Hallelujah! Christ is Risen,* 1862
8. Joshua 24:6 ff
9. *We Plough the Fields and Scatter,* translated from German by Jane Montgomery Campbell,1861

10. Luke 18:7
11. Murray Perahia, quoted in interview here: https://www.freise.in/single-post/2018/12/24/Murray-Perahia-on-Bach
12. András Schiff quoted at: https://fernjazz.wordpress.com/category/piano/
13. Julian of Norwich, *Revelations of Divine Life*, 1373, The Thirteenth Revelation, Chapter 27
14. Pierre Teilhard de Chardin, *On Love*, 1972
15. Imogen Cooper, *Soul Music*, BBC Radio 4, 9 January 2019
16. William Blake, *Auguries of Innocence*
17. Catherine Phillips, Fellow English at Downing College, Cambridge, on BBC *In Our Time*, 21 March 2019
18. Gerard Manley Hopkins, *As Kingfishers Catch Fire*

Postscript

1. Christopher Epting, VIII Bishop of Iowa (Ret.), The Episcopal Church, published on www.ProgressiveChristianity.org

THE NEW OPEN SPACES

Throughout the two thousand years of Christian tradition there have been, and still are, groups and individuals that exist in the margins and upon the edge of faith. But in Christianity's contrapuntal history it has often been these outcasts and pioneers that have forged contemporary orthodoxy out of former radicalism as belief evolves to engage with and encompass the ever-changing social and scientific realities. Real faith lies not in the comfortable certainties of the Orthodox, but somewhere in a half-glimpsed hinterland on the dirt track to Emmaus, where the Death of God meets the Resurrection, where the supernatural Christ meets the historical Jesus, and where the revolution liberates both the oppressed and the oppressors.

Welcome to Christian Alternative... a space at the edge where the light shines through.

If you have enjoyed this book, why not tell other readers by posting a review on your preferred book site.

Recent bestsellers from Christian Alternative are:

Bread Not Stones
The Autobiography of An Eventful Life
Una Kroll
The spiritual autobiography of a truly remarkable woman and a history of the struggle for ordination in the Church of England.
Paperback: 978-1-78279-804-0 ebook: 978-1-78279-805-7

The Quaker Way
A Rediscovery
Rex Ambler
Although fairly well known, Quakerism is not well understood. The purpose of this book is to explain how Quakerism works as a spiritual practice.
Paperback: 978-1-78099-657-8 ebook: 978-1-78099-658-5

Blue Sky God
The Evolution of Science and Christianity
Don MacGregor
Quantum consciousness, morphic fields and blue-sky thinking about God and Jesus the Christ.
Paperback: 978-1-84694-937-1 ebook: 978-1-84694-938-8

Celtic Wheel of the Year
Tess Ward
An original and inspiring selection of prayers combining Christian and Celtic Pagan traditions, and interweaving their calendars into a single pattern of prayer for every morning and night of the year.
Paperback: 978-1-90504-795-6

Christian Atheist

Belonging without Believing

Brian Mountford

Christian Atheists don't believe in God but miss him: especially the transcendent beauty of his music, language, ethics, and community.

Paperback: 978-1-84694-439-0 ebook: 978-1-84694-929-6

Compassion Or Apocalypse?

A Comprehensible Guide to the Thoughts of René Girard

James Warren

How René Girard changes the way we think about God and the Bible, and its relevance for our apocalypse-threatened world.

Paperback: 978-1-78279-073-0 ebook: 978-1-78279-072-3

Diary Of A Gay Priest

The Tightrope Walker

Rev. Dr. Malcolm Johnson

Full of anecdotes and amusing stories, but the Church is still a dangerous place for a gay priest.

Paperback: 978-1-78279-002-0 ebook: 978-1-78099-999-9

Do You Need God?

Exploring Different Paths to Spirituality Even For Atheists

Rory J.Q. Barnes

An unbiased guide to the building blocks of spiritual belief.

Paperback: 978-1-78279-380-9 ebook: 978-1-78279-379-3

Readers of ebooks can buy or view any of these bestsellers by clicking on the live link in the title. Most titles are published in paperback and as an ebook. Paperbacks are available in traditional bookshops. Both print and ebook formats are available online.

Find more titles and sign up to our readers' newsletter at http://www.johnhuntpublishing.com/christianity
Follow us on Facebook at
https://www.facebook.com/ChristianAlternative